PENGUIN BOOKS

THE RULE OF LAW

Tom Bingham, 'the most eminent of our judges' (*Guardia*
office successively as Master of the Rolls, Lord Chief Justice
land and Wales and Senior Law Lord of the United Kingdom, t
person ever to hold all three offices. He became a life peer, as
Bingham of Cornhill in the County of Powys, on becoming
Chief Justice in 1996. In 2005 he was appointed a Knight of th
ter, the first professional judge to be so honoured. He retired in
and in the same year was elected by the Institut de France as the nrst
winner of the Prize for Law awarded by the Alexander S. Onassis
Public Benefit Foundation. Tom Bingham died in September 2010,
six months after the first publication of this book.

The Bingham Centre for the Rule of Law was established in 2010, with
Lord Bingham's support, as part of the British Institute of International
and Comparative Law, and strives to support the development and
strengthening of the rule of law as set out in this book.

The Rule of Law was chosen as a 'book of the year' by Chris Patten
(in the *Observer*), Gideon Rachman (in the *Financial Times*) and Geoffrey Robertson (in the *New Statesman*).

TOM BINGHAM

The Rule of Law

PENGUIN BOOKS

PENGUIN BOOKS

Published by the Penguin Group
Penguin Books Ltd, 80 Strand, London WC2R 0RL, England
Penguin Group (USA) Inc., 375 Hudson Street, New York, New York 10014, USA
Penguin Group (Canada), 90 Eglinton Avenue East, Suite 700, Toronto, Ontario,
Canada M4P 2Y3 (a division of Pearson Penguin Canada Inc.)
Penguin Ireland, 25 St Stephen's Green, Dublin 2, Ireland (a division of Penguin Books Ltd)
Penguin Group (Australia), 250 Camberwell Road, Camberwell, Victoria 3124, Australia
(a division of Pearson Australia Group Pty Ltd)
Penguin Books India Pvt Ltd, 11 Community Centre, Panchsheel Park,
New Delhi – 110 017, India
Penguin Group (NZ), 67 Apollo Drive, Rosedale, Auckland 0632, New Zealand
(a division of Pearson New Zealand Ltd)
Penguin Books (South Africa) (Pty) Ltd, 24 Sturdee Avenue, Rosebank, Johannesburg 2196, South Africa

Penguin Books Ltd, Registered Offices: 80 Strand, London WC2R 0RL, England

www.penguin.com

First published by Allen Lane 2010
Published in Penguin Books 2011

014

Copyright © Tom Bingham, 2010

Typeset by Jouve (UK), Milton Keynes
Printed in England by Clays Ltd, St Ives plc

ISBN: 978-0-141-03453-9

www.greenpenguin.co.uk

MIX
Paper from
responsible sources
FSC™ C018179

Penguin Books is committed to a sustainable
future for our business, our readers and our planet.
This book is made from Forest Stewardship
Council™ certified paper.

Contents

For Elizabeth

Preface

In 2006 I was asked to give the sixth Sir David Williams Lecture at the University of Cambridge. This is an annual lecture established in honour (not, happily, in memory) of a greatly respected legal scholar, leader and college head in that university. The organizers generously offered me a free choice of subject. Such an offer always poses a problem to unimaginative people like myself. We become accustomed at school and university to being given a subject title for our weekly essay, and it was rather the same in legal practice: clients came with a specific problem which they wanted answered, or appeared before the judge with a specific issue which they wanted (or in some cases did not want) resolved. There was never a free choice of subject matter.

I chose as my subject 'The Rule of Law'. I did so because the expression was constantly on people's lips, I was not quite sure what it meant, and I was not sure that all those who used the expression knew what they meant either, or meant the same thing. In any event, I thought it would be valuable to be made to think about the subject, the more so since the expression had recently, for the first time, been used in an Act of the British Parliament, described rather portentously as 'an existing constitutional principle'.

The legal correspondents of the leading newspapers largely ignored the lecture (save on one relatively minor point), understandably regarding it as old hat, and it certainly lacked the kind of outright criticism of the government which whets the appetite of legal correspondents. But Martin Kettle, writing in the *Guardian* on 25 November 2006, thought the subject of some importance and suggested 'we need leaders who better understand the rule of law'. (On the same day the newspaper carried a headline asking 'Is this judge the most revolutionary man in Britain?', having a couple of years earlier described me as 'the radical who is leading a new English revolution'. This would have surprised my former tutor, the distinguished historian Christopher Hill. But the headline question was left unanswered, and I should warn those who look to this book for a revolutionary action plan that they are doomed to disappointment.) Since then, interest in this subject has, I think, continued to grow, fortified by concerns about the interrelationship between the rule of law, human rights and civil liberties on the one hand and security against terrorist attack on the other. The subject is one which merits consideration at greater length than is possible in a lecture. But in this book I have drawn heavily on what I said in that lecture and in others.

This book, although written by a former judge, is not addressed to lawyers. It does not purport to be a legal textbook. It is addressed to those who have heard references to the rule of law, who are inclined to think that it sounds like a good thing rather than a bad thing, who wonder if it may not be rather important, but who are not quite sure what it is all about and would like to make up their minds.

I begin in Chapter 1 of Part I with a brief, general introduction to what the rule of law means to us in Britain and other liberal democracies today, and to why it is important. Chapter 2 identifies some historical milestones on the way to our current conception of the rule of law. In my choice of milestones I am highly selective and shamelessly Anglocentric. Others more learned than I would choose different historical events, and cast their net more widely. But I stand by my selection, eccentric though some of my choices may appear to be, because the British have a history in this field of which they have every reason to be immensely proud, and I do not think it is as well known as it should be. Those with limited time, short attention spans or quick bus rides to work may wish to skip Chapter 2 and go straight to Chapter 3, but I hope they will not, since I think it illuminates the present to understand how we got there (and anyway the history is rather interesting). Part II, comprising Chapters 3–10, is the heart of the book, and in these chapters I seek to break down my very general definition of the rule of law into its constituent parts. Part III covers two general topics. In Chapter 11, I consider the impact of terrorism on the rule of law: are the rules of the game changing, as Tony Blair suggested on

5 August 2005? In Chapter 12 I discuss the interaction of parliamentary supremacy and the rule of law: a knotty problem, since parliamentary supremacy and the rule of law are usually said to be the two fundamental principles underlying our constitution in the UK, but they may not be entirely harmonious bedfellows.

I am immensely indebted to all those who as academics or judges have contributed to discussion of this subject, and to counsel appearing in numerous cases who have sought to expound, rely on and uphold the rule of law. But my most particular thanks are due to Richard Moules, Matthew Slater and Nicholas Gibson, who, as my successive judicial assistants between 2005 and 2008, have done almost all the digging for material, and to Diana Procter, who has saved me down the years from many errors. None of them, of course, is responsible for my opinions, with which they may well disagree. I owe a special debt to Kate Simmonds, who, in her scenic eyrie above the River Wye, typed and retyped the manuscript of this book. I am lastly very grateful to Caroline Dawnay of United Agents for her help and encouragement, and to Stuart Proffitt of Penguin Books, who conceived the idea of the book and made many helpful suggestions.

I must, finally, plead for mercy on two counts. First, to avoid the cumbrous 'he or she' and 'his or hers', and the ungrammatical 'they' when used in the singular, I have mostly stuck to saying 'he' or 'his'. I hope that this will be understood in an unchauvinistic, gender-neutral, way. Secondly, I am conscious of referring, disproportionately, in endnote references, to cases in which I have been involved. These are the cases most familiar to me. Perhaps – I do not know – this was the reason Elisabeth Schwartzkopf gave when, appearing on *Desert Island Discs*, she chose to console herself during her solitary exile with an exclusive choice of her own recordings.

PART I

I

The Importance of the Rule of Law

Credit for coining the expression 'the rule of law' is usually given to Professor A. V. Dicey, the Vinerian Professor of English Law at Oxford, who used it in his book *An Introduction to the Study of the Law of the Constitution*, published in 1885. The book made a great impression and ran to several editions before his death and some after. But the point is fairly made that even if he coined the expression he did not invent the idea lying behind it. One author[1] has traced the idea back to Aristotle, who in a modern English translation[2] refers to the rule of law, although the passage more literally translated says: 'It is better for the law to rule than one of the citizens', and continues: 'so even the guardians of the laws are obeying the laws'. Another author[3] points out that in 1866 Mr Justice Blackburn (later appointed as the first Lord of Appeal in Ordinary, or Law Lord) said: 'It is contrary to the general rule of law, not only in this country, but in every other, to make a person judge in his own cause ...'.[4] The same author[5] points out that the expression 'The Supremacy of the Law' was used as a paragraph heading in 1867. So Dicey did not apply his paint to a blank canvas. But the enormous influence of his book did mean that the ideas generally associated with the rule of law enjoyed a currency they had never enjoyed before.

Dicey gave three meanings to the rule of law. 'We mean, in the first place,' he wrote, 'that no man is punishable or can lawfully be made to suffer in body or goods except for a distinct breach of law established in the ordinary legal manner before the ordinary courts of the land.'[6] Dicey's thinking was clear. If anyone – you or I – is to be penalized it must not be for breaking some rule dreamt up by an ingenious minister or official in order to convict us. It must be for a proven breach of the established law of the land. And it must be a breach established before the ordinary courts of the land, not a tribunal of members picked to do the government's bidding, lacking the independence and impartiality which are expected of judges.

Dicey expressed his second meaning in this way: 'We mean in the second place, when we speak of "the rule of law" as a characteristic of our country, not only that with us no man is above the law, but (which is a different thing) that here, every man, whatever be his rank or condition, is subject to the ordinary law of the realm and amenable to the jurisdiction of the ordinary tribunals.'[7] Thus no one is above the law, and all are subject to the same law administered in the same courts. The first is the point made by Dr Thomas Fuller (1654–1734) in 1733: 'Be you never so high, the Law is above you.'[8] So, if you maltreat a penguin in the London Zoo, you do not escape prosecution because you are Archbishop of Canterbury; if you sell honours for a cash reward, it does not help that you are Prime Minister. But the second point is important too. There is no special law or court which deals with archbishops and prime ministers: the same law, administered in the same courts, applies to them as to everyone else.

Dicey put his third point as follows:

There remains yet a third and a different sense in which 'the rule of law' or the predominance of the legal spirit may be described as a special attribute of English institutions. We may say that the constitution is pervaded by the rule of law on the ground that the general principles of the constitution (as for example the right to personal liberty, or the right of public meeting) are with us the result of judicial decisions determining the rights of private persons in particular cases brought before the courts; whereas under many foreign constitutions the security (such as it is) given to the rights of individuals results, or appears to result, from the general principles of the constitution.[9]

Dicey's dismissive reference to foreign constitutions would now find few adherents. But he was a man of his time, and was concerned to celebrate, like Tennyson,

A land of settled government,
    A land of just and old renown,

> Where Freedom slowly broadens down
> From precedent to precedent.　　　　　('You ask me, why . . .')

Thus he had no belief in grand declarations of principle (and would, I think, have had very mixed views on the Human Rights Act 1998[10]), preferring to rely on the slow, incremental process of common law decision-making, judge by judge, case by case.

Dicey's ideas continued to influence the thinking of judges for a long time,[11] and perhaps still do, but as time went on they encountered strong academic criticism. His foreign comparisons were shown to be misleading, and he grossly understated the problems which, when he wrote, faced a British citizen seeking redress from the government.[12] As the debate broadened, differing concepts of the rule of law were put forward until a time came when respected commentators were doubtful whether the expression was meaningful at all. Thus Professor Raz has commented on the tendency to use the rule of law as a shorthand description of the positive aspects of any given political system.[13] Professor Finnis has described the rule of law as '[t]he name commonly given to the state of affairs in which a legal system is legally in good shape'.[14] Professor Judith Shklar has suggested that the expression may have become meaningless thanks to ideological abuse and general over-use: 'It may well have become just another one of those self-congratulatory rhetorical devices that grace the public utterances of Anglo-American politicians. No intellectual effort need therefore be wasted on this bit of ruling class chatter.'[15] Thomas Carothers, in 2003, observed that 'There is also uncertainty about what the essence of the rule of law actually is'.[16] Professor Jeremy Waldron, commenting on the decision of the US Supreme Court in *Bush v Gore*[17] – the case which decided who had won the presidential election in 2000, and in which the rule of law had been invoked by both sides – recognized a widespread impression that utterance of those magic words meant little more than 'Hooray for our side'.[18] Professor Brian Tamanaha has described the rule of law as 'an exceedingly elusive notion' giving rise to a 'rampant divergence of understandings' and analogous to the notion of the Good in the sense that 'everyone is for it, but have contrasting convictions about what it is'.[19]

In the light of opinions such as these, it is tempting to throw up one's hands and accept that the rule of law is too uncertain and subjective an expression to be meaningful. But there are three objections to this course. The first is that in cases without number judges have referred to the rule of law when giving their judgments.[20] Thus in one case, concerned with an effective increase made by the Home Secretary in the term to be served by a young convicted murderer, Lord Steyn, sitting in the House of Lords, said: 'Unless there is the clearest provision to the contrary, Parliament must be presumed not to legislate contrary to the rule of law. And the rule of law enforces minimum standards of fairness, both substantive and procedural.'[21] In a very different kind of case concerned with appeals against decisions made on issues of town and country planning, Lord Hoffmann, also sitting in the House of Lords, said: 'There is however another relevant principle which must exist in a democratic society. That is the rule of law.'[22] Statements of this authority, and many others like them, cannot be dismissed as meaningless verbiage.

The second objection is that references to the rule of law are now embedded in international instruments of high standing. Thus the preamble to the Universal Declaration of Human Rights 1948 – the great post-war statement of principle associated with the name of Mrs Eleanor Roosevelt – described it as 'essential, if man is not to be compelled to have recourse, as a last result, to rebellion against tyranny and oppression, that human rights should be protected by the rule of law'. The European Convention of Human Rights 1950, of which the UK was the first signatory, referred to the governments of European countries as having 'a common heritage of political traditions, ideals, freedom and the rule of law . . .'. Article 6 of the Consolidated Version of the Treaty on European Union, to which the UK is also a party, provides: 'The Union is founded on the principles of liberty, democracy, respect for human rights and fundamental freedoms, and the rule of law, principles which are common to the Member States.' Thus there is a strong international consensus that the rule of law is a meaningful concept, and a rather important one at that. The 1996 Constitution of South Africa, declaring in clause 1 the values on which the Republic is founded, lists the 'Supremacy of the Constitution and the rule of law'. Although 'the rule of law' is, obviously, an English expression, familiar in the UK and in countries such as Ireland, the United States, Canada, Australia and New Zealand, whose law has been influenced by that of Britain, it is also meaningful in countries whose law is influenced by the jurisprudence of Germany, France, Italy, the Netherlands and Spain. In Germany, for instance, reference is made to the *Rechtstaat*, in France to the *État de droit*, which, literally translated, mean 'the law-governed state'.

The third objection is that reference is now made to the rule of law in a British statute. The Constitutional Reform Act 2005 provides, in section 1, that the Act does not adversely affect '(a) the existing constitutional principle of the rule of law; or (b) the Lord Chancellor's existing constitutional role in relation to that principle'. Under section 17(1) of the Act the Lord Chancellor must, on taking office, swear to respect the rule of law and defend the independence of the judges. So there we have it: the courts cannot reject as meaningless provisions deliberately (and at a late stage of the legislative process) included in an Act of Parliament, even if they were to sympathize with some of the more iconoclastic views quoted above, as few (I think) would.

The practice of those who draft legislation is usually to define exactly what they mean by the terms they use, so as to avoid any possibility of misunderstanding or judicial misinterpretation. Sometimes they carry this to what may seem absurd lengths. My favourite example is found in the Banking Act 1979 Appeals Procedure (England and Wales) Regulations 1979, which provide that: 'Any reference in these regulations to a regulation is a reference to a regulation contained in these regulations.' No room for doubt there. So one might have expected the Constitutional Reform Act to contain a definition of so obviously important a concept as the rule of law. But there is none. Did the draftsmen omit a definition because they thought that Dicey's definition was generally accepted, without cavil, and called for no further elaboration? Almost certainly not: parliamentary draftsmen are very expert and knowledgeable lawyers, whose teachers would have expressed scepticism about some features of Dicey's analysis. More probably, I think, they recognized the extreme difficulty of devising a pithy definition suitable for inclusion in a statute. Better by far, they might reasonably have thought, to omit a definition and leave it to the judges to rule on what the term means if and when the question arises for decision. In this way a definition could be forged not in the abstract but with reference to particular cases and it would be possible for the concept to evolve over time in response to new views and situations.

Once the existing constitutional principle of the rule of law had been expressly written into a statute, it was only a matter of time before it was relied on by a litigating party. This duly occurred, perhaps sooner than anyone expected, in a case challenging a decision of the Director of the Serious Fraud Office to stop an investigation into allegedly corrupt payments said to have been made by BAE Systems Ltd. to officials in Saudi Arabia. His decision was held by one court to be contrary to the rule of law, although the House of Lords ruled that it was not, and therefore did not have to rule on what the rule of law meant in that context.[23] But the question is bound to arise again, and the task of devising at least a partial definition cannot be avoided indefinitely. So I think we must take the plunge.

The core of the existing principle is, I suggest, that all persons and authorities within the state, whether public or private, should be bound by and entitled to the benefit of laws publicly made, taking effect (generally) in the future and publicly administered in the courts. This statement, as will appear in Chapters 3–10, is not comprehensive, and even the most ardent constitutionalist would not suggest that it could be universally applied without exception or qualification. There are, for example, some proceedings in which justice can only be done if they are not conducted in public, as where a manufacturer sues to prevent a trade competitor unlawfully using a secret and technical manufacturing process. But generally speaking any departure from the rule I have stated calls for close consideration and clear justification. My formulation owes much to Dicey, but I think it also captures the fundamental truth propounded by the great English philosopher John Locke in 1690 that 'Wherever law ends, tyranny begins'.[24] The same point was made by Tom Paine in 1776 when he said 'that in America THE LAW IS KING. For as in absolute governments the King is law, so in free countries the law ought to be King; and there ought to be no other.'[25]

None of this requires any of us to swoon in adulation of the law, let alone lawyers. Many people on occasion share the view of Mr Bumble in *Oliver Twist* that 'If the law supposes that ... the law is a ass – a idiot.' Many more share the ambition expressed by one of the rebels in Shakespeare's *Henry VI, Part II*, 'The first thing we do, let's kill all the lawyers.' Few would choose to set foot in a court at any time in their lives if they could avoid it, perhaps echoing an Italian author's description of courtrooms as 'gray hospitals of human corruption'.[26] As for the judges, the public entertain a range of views, not all consistent (one minute they are senile and out of touch, the next the very people to conduct a detailed and searching inquiry; one minute port-gorged dinosaurs imposing savage sentences on hapless miscreants, the next wishy-washy liberals unwilling to punish anyone properly for anything), although often unfavourable. But belief in the rule of law does not import unqualified admiration of the law, or the legal profession, or the courts, or the judges. We can hang on to most of our prejudices. It does, however, call on us to accept that we would very much rather live in a country which complies, or at least seeks to comply, with the principle I have stated than in one which does not. The hallmarks of a regime which flouts the rule of law are, alas, all too familiar: the midnight knock on the door, the sudden disappearance, the show trial, the subjection of prisoners to genetic experiment, the confession extracted by torture, the gulag and the concentration camp, the gas chamber, the practice of genocide or ethnic cleansing, the waging of aggressive war. The list is endless. Better to put up with some choleric judges and greedy lawyers.

2

Some History

In this chapter I discuss, in an impressionistic, episodic and highly selective way, what seem to me to be important historical milestones on the way to the rule of law as we know it today.

(1) Magna Carta 1215

My point of embarkation is Magna Carta. Everyone has heard of this, the Great Charter. Some have set eyes on one or more of the three surviving originals in the British Library or Salisbury or Lincoln. It is very hard to decipher. It is in Latin. And even in translation much of it is very obscure and difficult to understand. But even in translation the terms of chapters 39 and 40 have the power to make the blood race:

39. No free man shall be seized or imprisoned or stripped of his rights or possessions, or outlawed or exiled, or deprived of his standing in any other way, nor will we proceed with force against him, or send others to do so, except by the lawful judgment of his equals or by the law of the land.
40. To no one will we sell, to no one deny or delay right or justice.

These are words which should be inscribed on the stationery of the Ministry of Justice and the Home Office, in place of the rather vapid slogans which their letters now carry.

Magna Carta was annulled by the Pope within a few months, on the ground that it had been exacted from King John by duress, and it has given rise to much bad history. It was not at that stage a statute, since there was nothing recognizable as a parliament. It did not embody the principles of jury trial, which was still in its infancy, or habeas corpus, which in its modern form had yet to be invented.[1] The language of chapter 39 has been criticized as 'vague and unsatis-factory',[2] and it has been said that chapter 40 'has had much read into it that would have astonished its framers'.[3] It would, moreover, be a travesty of history to regard the barons who confronted King John at Runnymede as altruistic liberals seeking to make the world a better place. But, for all that, the sealing of Magna Carta was an event that changed the constitutional landscape in this country and, over time, the world.

There were four main reasons for this. First, and in contrast with other European charters of the period, including the Golden Bull of Hungary of 1222, it was a grant to all free men throughout the realm.[4] Of course, not all men (or women) at the time were free. But to an exceptional degree it assumed a legal parity among all free men, thus contributing to a sense of community which may, perhaps, help to explain Britain's happy freedom from bloody revolution since its civil war 350 years ago.

Secondly, and contrary to the impression given by some elementary history books, the charter was not an instant response to the oppres-sion and exactions of a tyrannous king. It is true that during the reign of King John the country did experience what later came to be called 'the smack of firm government'. It is also true that his domestic dif-ficulties were exacerbated by his dispute with the Church and his military failures. But the roots of Magna Carta went much deeper. It drew heavily on earlier models, not least King Henry I's charter of liberties and the coronation oaths of previous kings. The charter of Henry I, issued on his accession to the throne in 1100 as a sort of non-election manifesto, promised relief from the evil custom and oppres-sive taxation of the previous reign, but also forbade the imposition of excessive penalties and required that penalties should fit the crime, reflecting the nature of the offence. The coronation oath included a promise to exercise justice and mercy in all judgments, an oath still (with minor modifications) prescribed by section 3 of the Coronation Oath Act 1688 and sworn by Queen Elizabeth II in 1953. Leading authorities are agreed. Dr McKechnie has written:

Looking both to the contents and the formalities of execution of John's Great Charter, the safer opinion would seem to be that, like the English Constitution, it is of mixed origin, deriving elements from ancestors of more races than one; but that the traditional line of descent from the oaths and writs of Anglo-Saxon kings, through the Charter of Henry I, is one that cannot be neglected.[5]

To the same effect, Sir James Holt, the greatest modern authority on the charter, has written: 'Magna Carta was not a sudden intrusion into English society and politics. On the contrary, it grew out of them ... Laymen had been assuming, discussing and applying the principles of Magna Carta long before 1215. They could grasp it well enough.'[6] This is important. Magna Carta was not a peace accord botched up to meet a sudden crisis and, as history repeatedly shows, liable to unravel. It had a quality of inherent strength because it expressed the will of the people, or at any rate the articulate representatives of the people.

Thirdly, the Charter was important because it represented and expressed a clear rejection of unbridled, unaccountable royal power, an assertion that even the supreme power in the state must be subject to certain overriding rules. Only by transporting ourselves imaginatively to the early thirteenth century can we appreciate how big a step this was. Today in the UK we speak of the supreme legislative authority as the Queen in Parliament, of the executive as Her Majesty's Ministers and of the judiciary as Her Majesty's Judges, and this is legally correct. But we know that the Queen has no choice but to assent to legislation duly laid before her, and that she has no power personally to hire or fire her ministers or her judges. In 1215 it was different. These powers, legislative, executive and judicial, really were concentrated in the King, the Lord's Anointed. But he became subject to the constraint of the law. That is why Magna Carta was such a significant watershed. There, clearly recognizable, was the rule of law in embryo.

But, fourthly, the significance of Magna Carta lay not only in what it actually said but, perhaps to an even greater extent, in what later generations claimed and believed it had said. Sometimes the myth is more important than the actuality. It has been said that 'Getting its history wrong is part of being a nation.'[7] So it was with Magna Carta. The myth proved a rallying point for centuries to come – and still does, for example when a government proposes some restriction of jury trial. And its influence is not purely local. An American author, writing in 1991, calculated that more than 900 federal and state courts in the United States had cited Magna Carta. In the half-century between 1940 and 1990, the Supreme Court had done so in more than sixty cases.[8]

(2) Habeas corpus: the challenge to unlawful detention

My second milestone is the old writ of habeas corpus or, to give the writ its full name (betraying its venerable origin), habeas corpus ad subjiciendum. The issue of a writ to secure the presence in court of a defendant or criminal suspect was familiar by the early thirteenth century, a welcome sign that even at that stage judges preferred to make orders when the party to be charged was before them.[9] But it was not then used to protect the liberty of the subject or investigate the lawfulness of a person's detention. That came later, when the writ was issued with another writ seeking an order of certiorari (now called a quashing order), and its development owed much to a competitive struggle for business between the courts administering the common law, the Court of Chancery administering its equity jurisdiction and the Court of High Commission, a royal prerogative court acting directly on behalf of the Crown.[10] The substantive remedy of habeas corpus was not, as already observed, a product of Magna Carta, but over time, however unhistorically, it came to be seen as such. Thus we can accept the truth of Sir William Holdsworth's judgment concerning the protection of liberty in the UK: 'Without the inspiration of a general principle with all the prestige of Magna Carta behind it, this development could never have taken place; and equally, without the translation of that principle into practice, by the invention of specific writs to deal with cases of infringement, it could never have taken practical shape.'[11]

The procedure was (and is) essentially simple. An unfortunate person (let us call him A.B.) finds himself languishing in Her Majesty's Prison at (let us say) Carlisle. He believes that he is, for whatever reason, detained unlawfully. So he procures the issue of a writ addressed to the Governor of Carlisle Prison which, in its modern form (the Latin version having been discarded), commands him to have the body of A.B. before a judge or divisional court at the Royal Courts of Justice in the Strand 'together with the day and cause of his being taken and detained, that the Court may examine and determine whether such cause is legal'.

Thus the essence of the old writ (literally, 'that you have the body') is preserved, and the Governor must appear in court, confirm that A.B. is in his custody, state when A.B. was so detained and, crucially, show good legal cause for detaining him, usually a valid order of a court. If he shows good legal cause, A.B. will continue to languish where he is. If he does not, the judge will order A.B. to be released. I have taken the example of a prisoner detained, as he thinks unlawfully, in prison. But the procedure is equally applicable to, for example, a patient compulsorily committed, unlawfully as he thinks, to a mental hospital, the writ in this instance being directed to the superintendent or hospital trust.

In *Bushell's Case*, decided in 1670, Chief Justice Vaughan was able to assert as simple fact: 'The writ of habeas corpus is now the most usual remedy by which a man is restored again to his liberty, if he have been against law deprived of it.'[12] The simplicity of the writ is its strength and its virtue. It has been widely recognized as the most effective remedy against executive lawlessness that the world has ever seen, a remedy introduced and developed by the judges and adopted elsewhere, notably in the United States. Thus a person may not be detained against his will on the say-so of a dictator or minister or official, unless such direction has the authority of law. He cannot be detained on the unlawful order of a judge either, although such an order is ordinarily challenged by appeal.

(3) The abolition of torture

Elementary textbooks on the history of medieval England, if of a certain vintage, used to contain pictures and descriptions of trial by ordeal: the suspect was required to hold a piece of molten iron, or was immersed in water, and if he survived without septicaemia or drowning God was held to have intervened to demonstrate his innocence. In an age of belief the practice had a certain logic, and a similar belief has its adherents even now in time of war. But the Lateran Council of 1215 condemned the practice as cruel. So both in England and Wales and in continental Europe other arrangements had to be made. Different procedures were chosen.

The procedure adopted in England and Wales was the precursor of jury trial as we know it today. The defendant was put before a jury and evidence was called against him. One witness, if believed, was enough. The defendant could not himself testify, but could call witnesses if he had any. The jury decided whether he was guilty or not. The procedure followed in continental Europe was very different. The Roman-canon models adopted there required that, to convict the defendant, there must be two witnesses, one corroborating the other, or else a confession. The practical problem was that two witnesses were frequently unavailable and the defendant chose not to confess. So, to overcome the latter difficulty, the authorities resorted to torture to force the defendant to confess, not as an exceptional or isolated occurrence but as a routine regularly followed.

The significance of this history for present purposes is that from a very early date, not later than the fifteenth century, the common law of England (the law made and administered by the judges, case by case, in the ordinary courts) adamantly set its face against the use of torture and the admission of evidence procured by torture.[13] Its rejection of this abhorrent practice was indeed hailed as a distinguishing feature of the common law, and was the subject of proud claims by a series of the greatest English legal writers, including Fortescue, Coke and Blackstone, who contrasted it with the practice adopted in Europe. The English rejection of torture was also the subject of admiring comment by authorities such as Voltaire. In rejecting the use of torture, whether applied to potential defendants or potential witnesses, the common law courts were moved by three considerations: the cruelty of the practice as applied to those unconvicted of any crime; the inherent unreliability of the evidence in confessions so procured, since a person subjected to unbearable pain will say anything which will cause the pain to stop; and a belief that the practice degraded all who had anything to do with it, including the courts if they received or relied on the fruits of such treatment.

Despite this rejection of torture by the common law courts, the practice of torture continued in England in the sixteenth and early seventeenth centuries. But this took place pursuant to warrants issued by the royal Council on behalf of the Crown, very largely in relation to alleged offences against the state (such as that committed by Guy Fawkes), in exercise of the royal prerogative and in what were called the royal prerogative courts, most notoriously the Court of Star Chamber. The exercise of this power became one of the important issues in the struggle between the Crown and the parliamentary common lawyers, since to the latter torture was, in the words of one authority, 'totally repugnant to the fundamental principles of English law' and 'repugnant to reason, justice, and humanity'.[14] While the history is uncertain, and the myth may again be more important than the actuality, the common law opponents of torture received a fillip from what was believed to have happened. A naval officer named John Felton fatally stabbed George Villiers, the Duke of Buckingham and Lord High Admiral of England, in August 1628. The Duke had been a favourite of King James I and was an intimate friend of King Charles I, who, it is said, consulted the judges whether Felton could be put to the rack to reveal his accomplices. The story is that the judges, having met, answered that Felton 'ought not by the law to be tortured by the rack, for no such punishment is known or allowed by our law'.[15] Whatever the truth of this story, it is certain that one of the very first acts of the Long Parliament in 1640 was to abolish the Court of Star Chamber, in which evidence obtained by torture was received, and since then no torture warrant has been issued in England. By one of the first enactments of the Westminster Parliament following the Act of Union in 1707, Scotland followed suit. But in continental Europe the practice continued for many years: drawings survive of handsome young men in wigs and fine stockings inflicting horrific torments on their bound victims. In France, torture was abolished in 1789; in different parts of Italy, between 1786 (Tuscany) and 1859 (Naples); in Prussia, torture was effectively abolished in 1740, but not formally until 1805; in Baden it continued until 1831; in the Netherlands it was abolished between 1787 and 1798; in Sweden it was forbidden in 1734 but occasionally inflicted later; Denmark abolished the practice in 1771; Russia abolished torture in 1801, but it was used on occasion until 1847. In the United States, torture was proscribed, from 1791 onwards, by the constitutional prohibition of cruel or unusual punishment (see below).

What has this got to do with the rule of law? A good deal, I suggest. It was early recognition that there are some practices so abhorrent as not to be tolerable, even when the safety of the state is said to be at risk, even where the price of restraint is that a guilty man may walk free. There are some things which even the supreme power in the state should not be allowed to do, ever.

(4) The Petition of Right 1628

My next milestone, the Petition of Right 1628, is a lineal descendant of Magna Carta and habeas corpus and is perhaps as important a contributor to the rule of law as either. Its genesis has been the subject in recent years of acute scholarly controversy,[16] and much of the detailed history is debatable. But the broad picture is reasonably clear. Moved by hostility to the Duke of Buckingham, the House of Commons in 1625 and 1626 denied Charles I the means to conduct military operations abroad which Buckingham was to command. The King was unwilling to give up his military ambitions and resorted to the expedient of a forced loan to finance it. A number of those subject to this imposition declined to pay, and some were imprisoned, among them those who became famous as 'the Five Knights': Sir Thomas Darnel, Sir John Corbet, Sir Walter Erle, Sir John Heveningham and Sir Edmund Hampden. Each of them sought a writ of habeas corpus to secure his release. Sir Thomas Darnel was rebuffed at an early stage and gave up the fight. The other four fought on, each represented by eminent counsel, who included John Selden. Their hope was that non-payment of the loan would be given as the reason for their imprisonment, whereupon the lawfulness of the loan could be challenged and investigated in court. But the Crown frustrated this hope by stating that the initial commitment and continued detention of the knights was 'per speciale mandatum domini regis', by his majesty's special commandment. Four King's Bench judges, headed by the Chief Justice, before whom the matter came had no knowledge, judicially, of why the knights were in prison, and made a simple order (with no final judgment) remanding the knights back to prison.

This proceeding was not as novel, or perhaps as shocking, as the subsequent furore might lead one to infer. The judges' order was, it seems, a provisional (not a final) refusal of bail and followed a familiar form. Those detained were released once the collection of the loan was complete, shortly after the hearing, and this may always have been the intention. Detention at the instance of the executive without charge or trial was not without precedent at the time. But the Commons, when they assembled in 1628, had no appetite for points like these. It was, as Conrad Russell has written, 'a one-issue Parliament'. It had 'the conscious and deliberate aim of vindicating English liberties'.[17] The outcome of the *Five Knights' Case* was one of the issues which fired this determination. Allied with it were the expropriation of personal property, by means of a forced loan, without parliamentary sanction; the billeting of soldiers; and resort to martial law. The parliamentary leadership – a formidable body including Sir Edward Coke, Sir John Eliot, John Pym, John Selden, Edward Littleton, Sir Nathaniel Rich, Sir Robert Phelips, Sir Dudley Digges, Sir John Glanville and others – saw the action of the Crown in these areas as a threat to that ideal of liberty which they claimed as a birthright. And the disquiet to which the decision in the *Five Knights' Case* gave rise is not hard to understand: for even if it was no more than a provisional decision on bail, the question inevitably arose whether the power of the King to detain without charge or trial was subject to any legal constraint, and if so what.

As is normal in such situations, both sides claimed to be defending the status quo. The leaders of the Commons invoked Magna Carta and later precedents, disavowing reliance on any novel principle. The King for his part declared his loyalty to old laws and customs, while resisting any surrender of his existing prerogative. But in truth the Commons were seeking to establish, more clearly and comprehensively than ever before, the supremacy of the law. On 26 April 1628, Sir Thomas Wentworth, a moderate influence in the Commons, expressed the hope that 'it shall never be stirred here whether the King be above the law or the law be above the King'.[18] But that was the very issue the majority wanted to resolve, in favour of the law. They had not only political reasons for seeking that outcome but also, with many common lawyers prominent among them, professional reasons. For if one of the ingredients of these debates was distrust of the King, another was doubt about the capacity of the common law to protect the subject. 'If this be law,' asked Sir Robert Phelips on 22 March 1628, 'what do we talk of our liberties?'[19] The leadership chose to restore trust in the law, and that precluded any workable settlement with the King.[20]

Thus it was that the Petition of Right came to be accepted by a reluctant Lords and eventually, on 7 June 1628, an even more reluctant King, who shortly thereafter sought to qualify his unqualified assent. Remarkably, although only in form a petition, this instrument was treated and printed as a statute.[21] Having invoked Magna Carta and the reference to due process in the revised version of Magna Carta enacted in 1354, clause V provided:

Nevertheless against the tenor the said statutes and other the good laws and statutes of your realm to that end provided, divers of your subjects have of late been imprisoned without any cause shown; and when for their deliverance they were brought before your justices by your Majesty's writ of habeas corpus there to undergo and receive as the Court should order, and their Keepers commanded to certify the causes of their detainer, no cause was certified, but that they were detained by your Majesty's special command signified by the lords of your Privy Council, and yet were returned back to several prisons without being charged with any thing to which they might make answer according to the law.[22]

And the conclusion came in clause VIII:

They do therefore humbly pray your most excellent majesty that no man hereafter be compelled to make or yield any gift, loan, benevolence, tax or such like charge without common consent by act of parliament, and that none be called to make answer or take such oath or to give attendance or be confined or otherwise molested or disquieted concerning the same or for refusal thereof. And that no freeman in any such manner as is before mentioned be imprisoned or detained. And that your Majesty would be pleased to remove the said soldiers and mariners, and that your people may not be so burdened in time to come. And that the aforesaid commissions for proceeding by martial law may be revoked and annulled. And that hereafter no commissions of like nature may issue forth to any person or persons whatsoever to be executed as aforesaid, lest by colour of them any of your Majesty's subjects be destroyed or put to death contrary to the laws and franchises of the land.

If there is one moment when the rule of law may be said to have come of age, the acceptance of the Petition of Right, for me, is it.

(5) Sir Matthew Hale's resolutions

My fifth milestone is not a great historical event, indeed not a historical event at all. It is the sort of resolution which many people make from time to time, even when it is not New Year: to get up earlier, work harder, take more exercise, drink less, or whatever. Dr Johnson was much given to resolutions of this kind. Sometimes we write these resolutions down, and sometimes they relate to how we do our jobs, as if we are trying to hold ourselves up to the mark by creating a semi-permanent record.

A surviving example of this practice is Sir Matthew Hale's list of 'Things Necessary to be Continually had in Remembrance'. Hale was Chief Justice of the King's Bench from 1671 to 1676 and his list dates from the 1660s, being rules composed by him to guide his own conduct as a judge. Some of his precepts have more resonance to modern ears than others, but I set out the list in full as Hale wrote it:

1. That in the administration of justice, I am entrusted for God, the King and Country; and therefore
2. That it be done (1) Uprightly (2) Deliberately (3) Resolutely.
3. That I rest not upon my own understanding or strength, but implore and rest upon the direction and strength of God.
4. That in the execution of justice, I carefully lay aside my own passions, and not give way to them however provoked.
5. That I be wholly intent upon the business I am about, remitting all other cares and thoughts as unseasonable and interruptions.
6. That I suffer not myself to be prepossessed with any judgment at all, till the whole business and both parties be heard.

7. That I never engage myself in the beginning of any cause, but reserve myself unprejudiced till the whole be heard.

8. That in business capital, though my nature prompts me to pity, yet to consider that there is also pity due to the country.

9. That I be not too rigid in matters purely conscientious, where all the harm is diversity of judgment.

10. That I be not biassed with compassion to the poor, or favour to the rich in point of justice.

11. That popular or court applause or distaste, have no influence into any thing I do in point of distribution of justice.

12. Not to be solicitous what men will say or think, so long as I keep myself exactly according to the rule of justice.

13. If in criminals it be a measuring cast, to incline to mercy and acquittal.

14. In criminals that consist merely in words when no more harm ensues, moderation is no injustice.

15. In criminals of blood, if the fact be evident, severity in justice.

16. To abhor all private solicitations of whatever kind soever and by whomsoever in matters depending.

17. To charge my servants (1) Not to interpose in any business whatsoever (2) Not to take more than their known fee (3) Not to give undue preference to causes (4) Not to recommend counsel.

18. To be short and sparing at meals that I may be fitter for business.

This list, made around 350 years ago, is significant because it lays down guidelines which would still today be regarded as sound rules for the conduct of judicial office. Hale recognized, as we would, that judges are servants of the public whose important work calls for their serious, single-minded, professional attention. He knew that he should try to exclude his personal feelings, avoid taking up any partisan position and suspend judgment until all the evidence and both parties had been heard. He acknowledged that in matters of life and death ('business capital') the interests of the criminal must be weighed against those of the public and the victim, and violent crimes might require severe penalties, but where the balance was even he inclined towards acquittal and mercy. His resolution was to do what was just, irrespective of public opinion. He would favour neither rich nor poor. He would receive no private representation concerning a pending case, and would keep the conduct of cases in his own personal hands.

These are standards to which modern judges still aspire. The judges are not, of course, the only guardians of the rule of law, perhaps not even the most important. Parliamentary and public opinion, informed by the media, should be alert to detect and scrutinize any infringement. But the judges' role in maintaining the rule of law is crucial, and Hale gave a valuable and relatively early indication of how they should perform their duties.

(6) The Habeas Corpus Amendment Act 1679

The Habeas Corpus Amendment Act 1679 would be a little-known footnote to history were it not for events taking place at Guantanamo Bay in Cuba between 2001 and 2009.

Following the restoration of the monarchy after the civil war and the Cromwellian Commonwealth, King Charles II's chief minister was the Earl of Clarendon. He, in the exercise of his executive powers, made a practice of dispatching prisoners to outlying parts of what is now the United Kingdom for the very reason that in those places the writ of habeas corpus did not run, because it was at the time a remedy local to England and Wales. Thus the prisoners were unable to challenge the lawfulness of their detention, as Clarendon intended that they should be. This was held to savour of unaccountable royal authority, and when Clarendon fell from power he was impeached. One of the charges against him was that he had sent persons to 'remote islands, garrisons, and other places, thereby to prevent them from the benefit of the law'.[23] Clarendon fled, and later died in exile. But opposition to this means of depriving prisoners of the protection of habeas corpus did not disappear with him.

Legislative measures to rectify this obvious abuse were adopted by the House of Commons on five occasions in the 1670s but on each occasion foundered in the Lords until, in 1679, a further comprehensive Habeas Corpus Amendment Act achieved a majority in that House also. The majority in the Lords was 57 to 55, and if Bishop Burnet (a contemporary historian) is to be believed, even that majority was only achieved because Lord Grey, acting as teller for the ayes, succeeded, without his opposite number noticing, in counting a very fat Lord as 10.[24] This attractive story may of course be apocryphal, but Sir William Holdsworth – by no means a frivolous author – describes the passage of the Bill as taking place 'under circumstances which lend some colour to Burnet's tale that the majority was arrived at by a miscount'.[25]

The motive of the United States Government in detaining terrorist suspects at Guantanamo Bay was exactly the same as Clarendon's: to deny them the remedy of habeas corpus provided in domestic law which, it was thought, could not be invoked by detainees held at an American military base in Cuba. Much litigation, and much suffering, would have been avoided had the rule of law been observed at Guantanamo from the start as it was required to be in the UK in 1679. Whether British officials contributed to the process by which some terrorist suspects ended up in Guantanamo is a question which has been asked but not yet answered.

(7) The Bill of Rights 1689 and the Act of Settlement 1701

The revolution of 1688–9, by which James II was expelled and replaced by William III (the Prince of Orange, imported from the Netherlands) and his wife Mary II (James's daughter), has earned the description 'glorious' because it was peaceful. No blood was shed. But for those tracing the development of the rule of law it was also glorious. Magna Carta and the Petition of Right delivered blunt messages that even kings are subject to the law. But King John had repudiated Magna Carta as soon as his immediate crisis was over, and Charles I had responded to the Petition of Right by ruling as an autocrat, without recourse to Parliament, for eleven years. In 1688–9 the message was less blunt, but the more effective for being so: William of Orange was offered the throne, but only if he was willing to accept the terms on which it was offered. There was a constitutional compact, not of the kind which political philosophers hypothesize but one negotiated between the prospective monarch and the political leaders of the day. It is known to history as the Bill of Rights 1689.

The flight of James II left the country without a parliament and without a king with authority to summon one. But what passed for the House of Commons appointed a committee of thirty-five members to draw up the terms on which, if he accepted them, William would become king. The committee worked with astonishing speed, drafting a declaration which was negotiated in detail with representatives of William and Mary before they finally accepted it, in the Banqueting House in Whitehall, on Wednesday, 13 February 1689.[26] Only then was the deal struck. It thereupon became possible for a parliament to be called, and the Bill of Rights, as agreed by William and Mary with minor amendments, was enacted into law. It received the royal assent on 16 December 1689.[27]

There is a tendency to think that conventions, charters and bills of rights are a modern development, and the Bill of Rights 1689 was only in part directed to the protection of individual rights. Its main focus was on the rules to which the Crown should be subject. Those rules were of immense and enduring importance. No monarch could again rely on divine authority to override the law.[28] The authority and independence of Parliament were proclaimed;[29] the integrity of its proceedings was protected[30] and there could be no standing army in time of peace without its sanction.[31] The power to suspend laws without the consent of Parliament was condemned as illegal.[32] So was the power of dispensing with laws or the execution of laws 'as it hath been assumed and exercised of late',[33] a provision which later legislation was intended to clarify,[34] but never did.[35] Personal liberty and security were protected by prohibiting the requirement of excessive fines,[36] the imposition of excessive bail,[37] and the infliction of 'cruel and unusual punishments'.[38] Jury trial was protected.[39] Modern readers will here discern the lineaments of the state in which they live.

But one thing was lacking. There is little advantage in the promulgation of laws, however benign, unless there are judges who are able and willing to enforce them. Otherwise, the powers that be can disregard the laws with impunity. But if the judges are to enforce the law against the highest authority in the state they must be protected against intimidation and victimization. The committee which drafted the Bill of Rights was alert to this point, and included in their first draft a provision safeguarding the tenure of the judges and protection of their salaries.[40] This, however, was dropped when it was decided (in the face of resistance by William of Orange) that the Bill should confirm old rights and not create new ones.[41] So it was necessary to defer this question until another day. That day came in 1701 when, in the Act of Settlement, Parliament legislated to provide for the Protestant succession to Queen Anne. The opportunity was then taken to enact the same provision as had been dropped in 1689,[42] which passed through both Houses without a division.[43] Coupled with a very much older rule which rendered the higher judiciary immune from civil suit or criminal prosecution for acts done in a judicial capacity,[44] the foundation of judicial independence was laid. For another sixty years the rule survived that judges need not be reappointed on the accession of a new monarch, and some were not.[45] Dr Johnson regretted the revocation of this rule. He pointed out that 'A Judge may become corrupt ... A Judge may become froward from age. A Judge may grow unfit for office in many ways. It was desirable that there should be a possibility of being delivered from him by a new King ...'.[46] At a time when judges could continue to serve indefinitely, Johnson's concern was understandable. But on this point, exceptionally, history has disagreed with him. A truly independent judiciary is one of the strongest safeguards against executive lawlessness; it thus becomes a victim of authoritarian governments, as the history of countries such as Zimbabwe and Pakistan graphically illustrates.

The lesson that even the supreme authority in the state is subject to the law was painfully learned. It cost one king his head and another his throne. But the Britain which emerged from the Glorious Revolution was one where the rule of law, imperfectly and incompletely, held sway.

(8) The Constitution of the United States of America

The Constitution of the United States was a crucial staging-post in the history of the rule of law. It was not the first attempt to draft a document laying down the respective powers and duties of the different institutions of government. Oliver Cromwell, with characteristic pre-science, had anticipated it (in the event, unsuccessfully) in his 1653 Instrument of Government. But the US Constitution was ground-breaking in its enlightened attempt to create a strong and effective central government while at the same time preserving the autonomy of the individual states and (in the first ten amendments) preserving the fundamental rights of the individual against what one contemporary commentator called 'the form of elective despotism'.[47] (Whether Lord Hailsham had this phrase in mind, consciously or unconsciously, when, in his 1976 Dimbleby Lecture, he made his much misquoted reference to 'elective dictatorship' can only, I think, be a matter of conjecture.[48]) The Constitution was also ground-breaking in being the product not of dictation by a ruling clique but of wide-ranging, very high quality debate and genuine democratic endorsement.

Most revolutionary of all, however, was the Constitution's enthrone-ment of the law. The preceding history helps to explain why this was done. The leaders of the American Revolution contained a number of prominent lawyers, well versed in the English common law and famil-iar with what, by this time, Magna Carta was believed to stand for. So, in resisting what they saw as the unlawful pretensions of the British Crown, it was natural for the colonists (like their English counterparts in the middle of the seventeenth century) to rely on the precedent of Magna Carta, treating it as a higher law which the Crown (it was argued) could not defy. It was a short step to providing, when adopting their own Constitution, that it should itself have the status of a higher law, unalterable without a strong popular mandate.

Article VI of the Constitution accordingly provided:

This Constitution, and the Laws of the United States which shall be made in pursuance thereof; and all Treaties made, or which shall be made, under the Authority of the United States, shall be the supreme Law of the Land; and the Judges in every State shall be bound thereby, any Thing in the Constitution or Laws of any State to the Contrary notwithstanding.

Thus the Congress (Article I), the President (Article II) and the federal judiciary (Article III) were to have such powers as were conferred by or under the Constitution, and none other. This contrasted, and continues to contrast, with the legislative omnipotence theoretically enjoyed by the Crown in Parliament in the UK (as more fully explained in Chapter 12 below). This point was fully appreciated, at any rate on the western side of the Atlantic, at the time. It was made by 'A Freeman' to the Freeholders and Freemen of Rhode Island on 20 March 1788. Of the British Parliament, the author correctly said: 'They are the supreme Legislative, their powers are absolute, and extend to an abolition of Magna Carta itself.'[49] The Congress was different: 'Their powers are not supreme, nor absolute, it being defined by the Constitution: and all powers therein not granted, are retained by State Legislatures.'[50] So, for the first time, I think, the law as expressed in the Constitution was to be supreme, binding not only the executive and the judges, but also the Legislature itself. Tom Paine was therefore right to say (see Chapter 1 above) 'that in America THE LAW IS KING'. This was indeed an advance for the rule of law, giving the law of the Constitution, as interpreted by the Supreme Court of the United States, an authority it had never before enjoyed anywhere.

(9) The French Declaration of the Rights of Man and the Citizen 1789

The French Declaration of the Rights of Man and the Citizen 1789 reflected the influence of Rousseau and other philosophers of the eighteenth-century Enlightenment. It was first drafted and put forward by the Marquis de Lafayette, who had returned from America inspired by the principles enshrined in the American Declaration of Independence. It declared that men were born and remained free and equal in rights; that the aim of all political association was to preserve the natural and imprescriptible rights of man; that sovereignty rested in the nation; that liberty consisted in freedom to do anything which was not injurious to others; that the law could only prohibit such actions as were harmful; that law was an expression of the general will; that no one should be accused or arrested or imprisoned except in cases and according to forms laid down by law; that the law should provide for only such punishments as were strictly and obviously necessary, and should not permit retrospective penalization; that as persons were held to be innocent until proved guilty, all unnecessary harshness in their initial treatment should be avoided; that no one should be harassed on account of his opinions and religious beliefs, provided they did not disturb public order; that the free communication of ideas was one of the most precious rights; that protection of the rights of man and the citizen required that there be military forces; that a common contribution to the expenses of the state was necessary; that there should be a right to vote on taxation; that society had the right to require public officials to account for their administrative acts; that a society in which the observance of the law was not assured, nor the separation of powers defined, had no constitution at all; and, finally, that since property was an inviolable and sacred right, no one was to be deprived of it save where public necessity demanded it, and then he should be compensated. Some of these provisions sound quite familiar to modern ears.

(10) The American Bill of Rights

The first ten amendments to the US Constitution, which took effect on 15 December 1791, have been known as the American Bill of Rights. It covers a lot of ground, some of it echoing the British Bill of Rights but some of it departing, deliberately, from the British model or going beyond it. Article I, framed to restrict the exercise of legislative power, provides that 'Congress shall make no law respecting an establishment of religion, or prohibiting the free exercise thereof; or abridging the freedom of speech, or of the press; or the right of the people peaceably to assemble, and to petition the government for a redress of grievances.' Article II lays down that 'A well regulated Militia, being necessary to the security of a free State, the right of the people to keep and bear Arms, shall not be infringed.' Article III is directed to the billeting of soldiers in time of peace and war, no doubt a live issue in the aftermath of the American Revolution. Article IV is of more general significance: 'The right of the people to be secure in their persons, houses, papers and effects, against unreasonable searches and seizures, shall not be violated, and no Warrants shall issue, but upon probable cause, supported by Oath or affirmation, and particularly describing the place to be searched, and the persons or things to be seized.' Thus, as in England, no general, unspecific, searches were to be authorized. Article V reflected British practice at that time, since modified in some respects:

No person shall be held to answer for a capital, or otherwise infamous crime, unless on a presentment or indictment of a Grand Jury, except in cases arising in the land or naval forces, or in the Militia, when in actual service in time of War or public danger; nor shall any person be subject for the same offence to be twice put in jeopardy of life and limb; nor shall be compelled in any criminal case to be a witness against himself, nor be deprived of life, liberty, or property, without due process of law; nor shall private property be taken for public use, without due compensation.

The expression 'due process', all but sacrosanct in American jurisprudence, derives from later translations of chapter 39 of Magna Carta (see (1) above). Article VI, again, both reflects and goes beyond British practice at the time:

In all criminal prosecutions, the accused shall enjoy the right to a speedy trial by an impartial jury of the State and district wherein the crime shall have been committed, . . . , and to be informed of the nature and cause of the accusation; to be confronted with the witnesses against him; to have compulsory process for obtaining witnesses in his favor, and to have the Assistance of Counsel for his defence.

The third of these rights, known to American lawyers as 'the confrontation clause', was an explicit rejection of the notoriously unfair procedure adopted at the trial of Sir Walter Raleigh for treason, when the Attorney General (Sir Edward Coke) adamantly refused to call the chief witness on whose evidence the prosecution relied, evidence which the witness had later retracted. Article VII preserves the right to trial by jury in any civil case where the sum in dispute exceeds twenty dollars. Article VIII, borrowed from the British Bill of Rights (see (7) above), provides: 'Excessive bail shall not be required, nor excessive fines imposed, nor cruel and unusual punishments inflicted.' Article IX provides for the retention of existing rights not enumerated in the Constitution, and Article X for the reservation to the States of powers not delegated to the Federal government by the Constitution. The

American Bill of Rights was the subject of a protracted struggle,[51] but the rights guaranteed in 1791 are rights which American citizens continue to enjoy.

(11) The law of war

I turn to a development of a rather different character, one not occurring at a single time or place and thus rather inaptly described as a milestone. It has taken effect over centuries, although with increasing momentum over the last century or so. I refer to the attempt to establish legally recognized standards of state conduct, even in relation to the use of force (the ius ad bellum, now governed by the United Nations Charter) and the conduct of war or armed conflict (the ius in bello). Rules to restrain the brutality inherent in war were familiar in classical times[52] and during the Middle Ages.[53] Both Richard II in 1385 and Henry V during the Agincourt campaign in 1415 issued ordinances to govern the conduct of their soldiers vis-à-vis the enemy.[54] Under the influence of writers such as Gentili (1552–1608)[55] and Grotius (1583–1645)[56] a body of customary international law began to grow up, fed by sources such as the 150 Articles of War signed by Gustavus Adolphus II of Sweden in 1621 and deriving its authority from the practice of the nations, regarded by them as a matter of obligation. On occasion such rules were the subject of bilateral treaty, as in the 1785 treaty between the United States and Prussia which, although a treaty of Amity and Commerce, contained provisions to be applied if war between them were to occur. Thus Article 23 defined the immunity of merchants, women, children, scholars, cultivators and others. Article 24 provided for proper treatment of prisoners of war, and began: 'And to prevent the destruction of prisoners of war by sending them into distant and inclement countries, or by crowding them into close and noxious places, the two contracting parties solemnly pledge themselves to each other and to the world that they will not adopt any such practice.'[57] During the American Civil War, Abraham Lincoln commissioned from Francis Lieber, and issued to the Northern army, a notably enlightened *Code of War for the Government of the Armies of the United States in the Field*. (Lieber was a professor of history at

Columbia: born in Berlin in 1800, he had served under Blücher as a teenager in 1815 and fought in the Greek War of Independence before emigrating to the United States in 1827.)

Over the last century and a half decisions of international courts and tribunals and the opinions of the learned have been influential in setting the standards of permissible conduct in war, but the scene has been dominated by a plethora of international conventions addressing different aspects of this multi-faceted subject. The history of these conventions yields a rich and diverse gallery of heroes, from whom any selection is to some extent invidious. But certain figures stand out. Among them is that of Jean-Henri Dunant, whose book *A Memory of Solferino*,[58] published in 1862, describing the horrific aftermath of that battle, which he had witnessed, inspired the first, 1864, Geneva Convention on Treatment of the Wounded[59] and the foundation of the International Committee of the Red Cross.[60] Also worthy of mention is Tsar Alexander II, who convened the conference which promulgated the 1868 St Petersburg Declaration Renouncing the Use, in Time of War, of Explosive Projectiles under 400 Grammes Weight, which were liable to cause cruel injuries but not kill, a declaration to which nineteen states assented.[61] The initiative of Alexander II was taken further by his grandson, Nicholas II, who convened the First Hague Peace Conference in 1899, which led to three conventions and three declarations. One of the declarations, to which Great Britain acceded despite initial objections, related to a type of bullet first manufactured at the British Indian arsenal of Dum-Dum, near Calcutta.[62] The Second Hague Peace Conference of 1907, convened at the instance first of President Theodore Roosevelt and then of Tsar Nicholas II also, was even more productive, giving rise to thirteen conventions and one declaration, most of them directed to the conduct of war on land and sea.[63] Among many conventions made after the Second World War under the auspices of the United Nations, special mention may be made of the 1948 United Nations Convention on the Prevention and Punishment of the Crime of Genocide, the eventual outcome of a request made to the Secretary-General by the delegations of Cuba, India and Panama.[64] In this much-abbreviated roll of honour I would also include Gustave Moynier, one of the founders of the International Committee of the Red Cross, who in 1872 urged the establishment of an international criminal court to adjudicate on violations of the 1864 Geneva Convention on Treatment of the Wounded. His wish was fulfilled on ratification of the 1998 Rome Statute of the International Criminal Court, although regrettably the United States, a strong supporter of the proposal in its earlier stages and a strong supporter of international criminal tribunals established for the former Yugoslavia and Rwanda in 1993 and 1994,[65] in the end refused to become a party, unwilling that its servicemen should be subject to the jurisdiction of a foreign court. It is easy to disparage all these rules as ineffective and difficult to enforce. Many people have done so. But to the extent that the rules have led to anyone – combatants, wounded, prisoners of war, women, children, civilians, non-combatants – being spared the full horror of unrestrained warfare, they must be accounted a victory for the rule of law.

(12) The Universal Declaration of Human Rights

My final milestone is the Universal Declaration of Human Rights, adopted by the General Assembly of the newly formed United Nations in Paris on 10 December 1948 with 48 votes in favour, eight abstentions[66] and no votes against. Contrary to the original wishes of the British and of René Cassin,[67] the influential French delegate and negotiator, the declaration was not (and is not) binding. But, drawing on Magna Carta, the Bill of Rights 1689, the French Declaration of the Rights of Man and the Citizen of 1789 and the American Bill of Rights, it has provided the common standard for human rights upon which formal treaty commitments have subsequently been founded, and has inspired the International Covenant on Civil and Political Rights 1966, the International Covenant on Economic, Social and Cultural Rights 1966, the International Covenant on the Elimination of All Forms of Racial Discrimination 1966 and regional treaties such as the European Convention on Human Rights 1950, the American Convention on Human Rights 1969, the African Charter on Human and Peoples' Rights 1981 and the Arab Convention on Human Rights 1994.[68]

The framers of the Universal Declaration sought, or received, advice from many sources, which included the Huxleys (Julian and Aldous),

H. G. Wells, Teilhard de Chardin and Benedetto Croce.[69] The paternity of the Declaration has been the subject of some controversy, and the contribution of René Cassin, though great, has perhaps been exaggerated.[70] In the judgment of John Humphrey, the distinguished Canadian international lawyer who prepared the first draft, the Declaration 'had no father' because 'literally hundreds of people ... contributed to its drafting'.[71] But the Declaration was, as Pope John XXIII was to say in his 1963 encyclical *Pacem in Terris*, 'an act of the highest importance' and the role of leadership was exercised by four people in particular: Eleanor Roosevelt, René Cassin, Charles Malik of Lebanon and P. C. Chang of China. If, as I think, the rule of law now demands protection of fundamental human rights, these four, more than any others, deserve credit for the almost worldwide acceptance of that principle and for the steps taken in many countries thereafter to make the principle enforceable and effective.[72]

PART II

3

The Accessibility of the Law

In Chapter 1, I identified what I described as the core of the existing principle of the rule of law: that all persons and authorities within the state, whether public or private, should be bound by and entitled to the benefit of laws publicly made, taking effect (generally) in the future and publicly administered in the courts. I then acknowledged that this principle, so stated, was not comprehensive and not universally applicable. In this and the following chapters I seek to explore the ingredients of the rule of law a little more thoroughly. I do so by advancing eight suggested principles. There is no magic about these. Others would come up with different principles, or would express these principles differently. But it is, I think, necessary to go behind the very general principle I have stated to try and identify what the rule of law really means to us, here and now.

(1) The law must be accessible and so far as possible intelligible, clear and predictable

Why must it?

I think there are really three reasons. First, and most obviously, if you and I are liable to be prosecuted, fined and perhaps imprisoned for doing or failing to do something, we ought to be able, without undue difficulty, to find out what it is we must or must not do on pain of criminal penalty. This is not because bank robbers habitually consult their solicitors before robbing a branch of the NatWest, but because many crimes are a great deal less obvious than robbery, and most of us are keen to keep on the right side of the law if we can. One important function of the criminal law is to discourage criminal behaviour, and we cannot be discouraged if we do not know, and cannot reasonably easily discover, what it is we should not do.

The second reason is rather similar, but not tied to the criminal law. If we are to claim the rights which the civil (that is, non-criminal) law gives us, or to perform the obligations which it imposes on us, it is important to know what our rights or obligations are. Otherwise we cannot claim the rights or perform the obligations. It is not much use being entitled to, for example, a winter fuel allowance if you cannot reasonably easily discover your entitlement, and how you set about claiming it. Equally, you can only perform a duty to recycle different kinds of rubbish in different bags if you know what you are meant to do.

The third reason is rather less obvious, but extremely compelling. It is that the successful conduct of trade, investment and business generally is promoted by a body of accessible legal rules governing commercial rights and obligations. No one would choose to do business, perhaps involving large sums of money, in a country where the parties' rights and obligations were vague or undecided. This was a point recognized by Lord Mansfield, generally regarded as the father of English commercial law, around 250 years ago when he said: 'The daily negotiations and property of merchants ought not to depend upon subtleties and niceties; but upon rules easily learned and easily retained, because they are the dictates of common sense, drawn from the truth of the case.'[1] In the same vein he said: 'In all mercantile transactions the great object should be certainty: and therefore, it is of more consequence that a rule should be certain, than whether the rule is established one way or the other. Because speculators [meaning investors and businessmen] then know what ground to go upon.'[2] But this is not an old-fashioned and outdated notion. Alan Greenspan, the former chairman of the Federal Reserve Bank of the United States, when recently asked, informally, what he considered the single most important contributor to economic growth, gave as his considered answer: 'The rule of law.' Even more recently, *The Economist* published an article which said: 'The rule of law is usually thought of as a political or legal matter ... But in the past ten years the rule of law has become important in economics too ... The rule of law is held to be not only good in itself, because it embodies and encourages a just society, but also as a cause of other good things, notably growth.'³ The article went on to acknowledge some dispute among economists about the strength of the connection between the rule of law and economic growth, drawing attention to China as an exception, but did not suggest there was no connection.

Given the importance of this principle, we cannot be surprised to find it clearly stated by courts all over the world. In the House of Lords in 1975 Lord Diplock said: 'The acceptance of the rule of law as a constitutional principle requires that a citizen, before committing himself to any course of action, should be able to know in advance what are the legal principles which flow from it.'⁴ He made much the same point a few years later: 'Elementary justice or, to use the concept often cited by the European Court [the Court of Justice of the European Communities], the need for legal certainty demands that the rules by which the citizen is to be bound should be ascertainable by him (or, more realistically, by a competent lawyer advising him) by reference to identifiable sources that are publicly available.'⁵ The European Court of Human Rights at Strasbourg has spoken to similar effect:

[T]he law must be adequately accessible: the citizen must be able to have an indication that is adequate in the circumstances of the legal rules applicable to a given case ... a norm cannot be regarded as a 'law' unless it is formulated with sufficient precision to enable the citizen to regulate his conduct: he must be able – if need be with appropriate advice – to foresee, to a degree that is reasonable in the circumstances, the consequences which a given action may entail.⁶

So too the Chief Justice of Australia, listing the practical conclusions held by Australian courts to be required by the principle of the rule of law: 'the content of the law should be accessible to the public'.⁷

So the question arises: how well is this rule observed today? The answer, of course, varies from country to country. In the countries of continental Europe, for example in Germany, France, Italy and the Netherlands, much of the law is found in compact, carefully drafted codes. In many common law countries (such as Australia) considerable effort has been devoted to trying to make legislation clear, succinct and intelligible. In Britain, the answer varies according to the source of the particular law under discussion. There are three main sources which call for consideration. They are, first, laws made by Parliament in duly enacted Acts of Parliament, to which must be added statutory instruments made by ministers or others in the exercise of authority conferred by Act of Parliament. Secondly, there is judge-made law, the decisions made by English or Welsh, Scots or Northern Irish judges laying down rules to govern their decisions in particular cases. The law so made, the common law, can be overridden by statute, but it has a long history, it has not lost its virility with age and in certain fields of law it is the dominant source. The third source is the law of the European Union, of which I say more below. It has effect here and overrides both statute and common law in the ever-growing areas to which it applies and is now an important source of law.

Statute law

On 11 July 2007 Sir Menzies Campbell, then the Liberal Democrat leader, pointed out in the House of Commons that during the past ten years there had been 382 Acts of Parliament, including ten Health Acts, twelve Education Acts and twenty-nine Criminal Justice Acts, and more than 3,000 new criminal offences had been created.[8] Professor Anthony King has drawn attention to a report published in 1992 which calculated that between 1979 and 1992 Parliament passed 143 Acts having a direct bearing on local government in England and Wales and that, of that total, no fewer than 53 effected some radical alteration to the existing system of local government.[9] In the year 2006 nearly 5,000 pages of primary legislation (Acts of Parliament) were enacted with in addition some 11,500 pages of subordinate legislation made by ministers. As Sir Menzies observed, 'The mantra might have been "Education, education, education" but the reality has been "Legislation, legislation, legislation".' It seems that legislative hyperactivity has become a permanent feature of our governance.

Is this other than a good thing? Those called upon to advise on recent legislative changes or apply them can, one might suppose, find out what they are by assiduous use of the internet, and the changes no doubt represent a parliamentary judgment of what will best serve the needs of the country. There is some force in both these points, but they do not dispel the concerns aroused, from a rule of law perspective, by the torrent of legislation which we have witnessed, particularly in the criminal field, in recent years. The Criminal Justice Act 2003 may be taken as a prime example. A highly experienced and knowledgeable criminal judge has described the provisions of the Act in one case as 'labyrinthine' and 'astonishingly complex'[10] and in another as 'deeply confusing', adding: 'We find little comfort or assistance in the historic canons of construction for determining the will of Parliament which were fashioned in a more leisurely age and at a time when elegance and clarity of thought and language were to be found in legislation as a matter of course rather than exception.'[11] Thus legislation of this kind poses real problems of assimilation and comprehension, even to senior and seasoned professionals. Part of the problem may lie in what a parliamentary committee criticized as 'the tendency of all governments to rush too much weighty legislation through Parliament in too short a time'.[12] Part of the problem may also lie in the traditional practice of British parliamentary draftsmen, which depends very heavily on cross-reference between provisions in a number of different Acts and statutory instruments, making it necessary for the reader to pursue what may be a long paper-chase through a series of legislative provisions. There is a price for all this. Changes in criminal law or procedure lead to a proliferation of appeals, and the Criminal Cases Review Commission, established to refer suspected miscarriages of justice back to the Court of Appeal, has described the complexity of recent sentencing provisions as a continuing source of references.[13] The biggest loser is, of course, the ordinary person who wants to try and find out, probably with professional help, what the law is.

A recent case illustrates the problems to which this legislative confusion gives rise.[14] A defendant was accused of a tobacco smuggling offence and pleaded guilty in 2007. A community sentence was imposed, and application was made for a confiscation order. His liability to a confiscation order depended on his having evaded payment of duty which he was personally liable to pay. To show that he was liable, the prosecution relied on some 1992 regulations. The trial judge was satisfied that he was liable, and ordered him to pay £66,120 or serve twenty months in prison if he did not. He appealed. The appeal came before three senior judges in the Court of Appeal, who heard argument and announced that they would give their judgment later in writing. They concluded that the defendant was liable to pay the duty under the 1992 regulations, and circulated a draft judgment upholding the confiscation order. On the eve of formally delivering judgment, however, they learned that the 1992 regulations no longer applied to tobacco products, as a result of different regulations made in 2001. Neither the trial judge, nor the prosecutor, nor defending counsel, nor the judges in the Court of Appeal knew of these later regulations, and they were not at fault. As Lord Justice Toulson said, giving judgment allowing the appeal:

there is no comprehensive statute law database with hyperlinks which would enable an intelligent person, by using a search engine, to find out all the legislation on a particular topic. This means that the courts are in many cases unable to discover what the law is, or was at the date with which the court is concerned, and are entirely dependent on the parties for being able to inform them what were the relevant statutory provisions which the court has to apply. This lamentable state of affairs has been raised by responsible bodies on many occasions . . .[15]

Reporting and commenting on this case in the *Guardian*, Marcel Berlins suggested that the age-old maxim might have to be revised: ignorance of the law is no excuse, unless there is no way of finding out what the law is.[16] This was plainly written in jest. But in 1988 and again in 1995 the Italian Constitutional Court ruled that ignorance of the law may constitute an excuse for the citizen when the formulation of the law is such as to lead to obscure and contradictory results.[17]

It must be questioned whether the current volume and style of legislation are well suited to serve the rule of law even if it is accepted, as it must be, that the subject matter of much legislation is inevitably very complex.

Judge-made law

The judges are quite ready to criticize the obscurity and complexity of legislation. But those who live in glass houses are ill-advised to throw stones. The length, elaboration and prolixity of some common law judgments (not just here but in other countries such as the United

States, Canada, Australia and New Zealand) can in themselves have the effect of making the law to some extent inaccessible.

Most cases decided by judges in court raise issues of fact but no issue of what the law is. Typical is the case where two motorists collide on a stretch of straight road and each accuses the other of driving on the wrong side of the road. The judge must do his or her best to decide where the truth lies, and is scarcely allowed to say 'Don't know', although the outcome may be that both drivers are held equally to blame. In such a case the facts are all-important, and may be hard to decide. The judge must give a judgment outlining the decision reached. But it is unlikely that any question of law will have to be decided. Often, however, a trial judge sitting alone at first instance will have to decide a question of law, and this is almost always so where a case comes before a Divisional Court (usually of two judges), a Court of Appeal (usually of three judges), or the House of Lords (usually a committee of five judges, but occasionally seven and exceptionally nine). All of these judges may give separate judgments, not saying exactly the same thing (or there would be no point in saying it) and sometimes disagreeing with each other. It is here that the problems of length, prolixity and elaboration – leading to inaccessibility – can arise.

The problem can be illustrated by reference to a question which the House of Lords has recently addressed on three separate occasions in the space of three years.[18] The question was whether, when a local authority seeks possession of premises which a person has occupied as his home, but which under our law applicable to tenancies and caravan sites he has no right to continue to occupy (because his tenancy has expired or he has been given notice to quit), he can seek to resist eviction by relying on the right to respect for his home protected by Article 8 of the European Convention on Human Rights, given effect here by the Human Rights Act 1998, as discussed in Chapter 7 below. The detached observer might suppose that the answer to the question would be 'yes' or 'no' or 'sometimes', and, if 'sometimes', would expect guidance to be given on when Article 8 could be relied on and when it could not. In the event, answering this question has provoked marked differences of opinion between the Court of Appeal and the House of Lords, and between the members of the House of

Lords themselves. In the House alone, the question has been addressed in fifteen separate reasoned judgments running to more than 500 paragraphs and more than 180 pages of printed law report. Even after this immense outpouring of effort it may be doubted whether the relevant law is entirely clear, or for that matter finally settled.

When the last of these three cases was before the Court of Appeal, that court, having struggled to give loyal effect to what the majority in the House of Lords had up to then decided (and, as the House was later to hold, reached the wrong answer), made a plea for a single judgment setting out the ruling of the majority. This would allow those who disagreed to say so and give their reasons for doing so, but (it was thought) give clearer and more intelligible guidance to lower courts on the law to be applied.

This is part of a wider debate on the form in which judgments can best be given, on which practice varies widely. In continental Europe the tradition is that the court speaks with a single authoritative voice, no dissent is permitted, and (notably in France) judgments are expressed very briefly, with minimal reasoning. Even in our own country the practice varies. Thus in the Court of Appeal (Criminal Division) there must be a single judgment, except where the presiding judge states that in his opinion the question is one of law on which it is convenient that separate judgments should be pronounced by members of the court,[19] a course which is never in practice adopted. So if one member of the court disagrees with the others, he or she must swallow any misgivings. This was for many years the practice in the Judicial Committee of the Privy Council, hearing appeals from the Empire and later the Commonwealth, the Isle of Man and the Channel Islands, although members who disagreed could record their dissent in a register which was never seen by anyone. Perhaps this salved their consciences. By contrast, in the civil appellate courts and in the House of Lords when hearing criminal appeals, the tradition has always been that any judge who wished to deliver a separate opinion could do so, and any judge who disagreed with his colleagues could say so. Despite this, the practice of the Court of Appeal has increasingly been to give a single judgment of the court in civil cases (it has been estimated[20] that almost one in three judgments nowadays is so given), and in recent years the House of Lords has on some occasions given a single considered opinion of the appellate committee.[21]

Those who favour multiple judgments and freedom to dissent do so because this practice fosters beneficial development of the law and avoids unsatisfactory compromises which result in a final judgment commanding the wholehearted support of no one. This is a view which has strong and authoritative supporters. It is not, in my opinion, a practice which undermines the rule of law, provided that two all-important conditions are observed.

The first is that, however many separate judgments are given and whether or not some members of the court dissent, the principle of law laid down by the court (or the majority of it) should be clear. It is only the principle of law laid down which binds any other court or governs any other case, and if the court does not make that principle clear it is simply failing to perform its duty in accordance with the principle now under discussion.

The second condition relates to the judges' role in developing the law. It used to be said that the judges did not make law but merely declared what the law had always been. This is a view which has few, if any, adherents today. Some judges, such as the late Lord Denning, are proud of their role in developing the law; most are more reticent. But cases are brought raising novel questions, and the judges have to answer them. Their answers will often make law, whatever answer they give, one way or the other. So the judges do have a role in developing the law, and the common law has grown up as a result of their doing just this. But, and this is the all-important condition, there are limits. The judges may not develop the law to create new criminal offences or widen existing offences so as to make punishable conduct of a type hitherto not subject to punishment,[22] for that would infringe the fundamental principle that a person should not be criminally punishable for an act which was not criminal when it was done.[23] In civil cases also we may agree with Justice Heydon of the High Court of Australia that judicial activism taken to extremes can spell the death of the rule of law:[24] it is one thing to move the law a little further along a line on which it is already moving, or to adapt it to accord with modern views and practices; it is quite another to seek to recast the law in a radically innovative or adventurous way, because that is to make it uncertain and unpredictable, features which are the antithesis of the rule of law. It is also, of course, very tough on the loser in the particular case, who has lost because the goalposts have been moved during the course of the litigation. This can, if the movement is substantial and unpredictable, offend the rule suggested earlier, that laws should generally take effect in the future.

The law of the European Union

When the UK acceded to the Treaty of Rome and became a member state of the European Communities (what was then called the Common Market), Parliament passed the European Communities Act 1972. That provided in effect that the law of the Communities should have effect in this country. The European Court of Justice was, and still is, the top supranational court of the Community, vested with authority to interpret the law, and it had already ruled in cases of fundamental importance that the provisions of the Treaty of Rome had direct effect in member states and that Community law enjoyed primacy over any inconsistent national law of a member state.[25] Where a national court is confronted by a question of Community law which must be resolved to decide the case, but to which the answer is not clear, it may (and in final courts of appeal must) refer the question to the European Court for a ruling on the point.[26] This procedure is not an appeal – it is for the national court to decide the case – but the Community law issue must be decided in accordance with the ruling of the European Court.

Thus the UK became bound to comply with the treaties and with European legislation made in regulations and directives, and with the decisions of the European Court, all of which became part of our own law, which the courts are bound to enforce. This is not problematical from a rule of law viewpoint, since (by Article 6 of the Treaty on European Union) the Union is founded on principles which include the rule of law. So no very detailed discussion is called for.

But European legislation and decisions do pose two problems for British courts seeking to give them effect. First, the legislation. This, inevitably given its provenance, is the work of draftsmen, drawn from the different member states, whose methods of working differ from those with which British courts are familiar, and who are seeking to formulate rules uniformly applicable in member states with very different institutions and traditions. It is not always possible, from a straightforward reading of a text, to be sure how it is intended to apply in a given case. This is often so where an international text has to be given effect in national law, and the text may well reflect the differing aims of different negotiators. But the problems are not insoluble, and in case of doubt the opinion of the European Court of Justice may be requested. Secondly, the decisions. The European Court, created in the continental European image, gives a single judgment, with no dissents. It is a fact of judicial life (as of human life more generally) that different minds react differently to the same problem, and this is the more likely to be so where a number of judges have been brought up in countries with different legal systems, cultures and traditions. The text of the single judgment will seek to accommodate the views of as many judges as possible, but the process of accommodation can lead to an undesirable blurring of lines and obfuscation of issues. Cases have arisen in which British courts, having received a ruling from the European Court on a reference, have been asked to make a further reference to seek a clarification of the ruling. It is clear that the point made above in the domestic context applies here also: no matter what the form of the judgment, the rule of law requires that the rule laid down should be clear.[27]

4

Law not Discretion

(2) Questions of legal right and liability should ordinarily be resolved by application of the law and not the exercise of discretion

Dicey was adamantly opposed to the conferment of discretionary decision-making powers on officials. This, he believed, opened the door to arbitrariness, which is the antithesis of the rule of law. His views were strongly endorsed some years later by the Lord Chief Justice of England (Lord Hewart) who, in a powerful and very readable polemic published in 1929 entitled *The New Despotism*, launched a coruscating attack on the legislative and administrative practices of the day. Particularly objectionable to him were the practices of authorizing ministers to amend or disapply an Act of Parliament, delegating decisions of a judicial nature to bureaucrats, and providing by statute that the decisions made by them should be immune from legal challenge. Wielding his pen like the journalist he had once been, Hewart wrote: 'It does not take a horticulturalist to perceive that, if a tree is bearing bad fruit, the more vigorously it yields the greater will be the harvest of mischief.'[1] He thought the tree was at the time bearing a great deal of bad fruit.

Lord Hewart gave many examples. One was section 67(1) of the Rating & Valuation Act 1925, which provided:

If any difficulty arises in connection with the application of this Act to any exceptional area, or the preparation of the first valuation list for any area, or otherwise in bringing into operation any of the provisions of this Act, the Minister [of Health] may by order remove the difficulty, or constitute any assessment committee, or declare any assessment committee to be duly constituted, or do any other thing which appears to him necessary or expedient for securing the preparation of the list or for bringing the said provisions into operation, and any such order may modify the provisions of this Act so far as may appear to the Minister necessary or desirable for carrying the order into effect.

Another example Hewart relied on was section 1(3) of the Town Planning Act 1925:

The expression 'land likely to be used for building purposes' shall include any land likely to be used as, or for the purpose of providing, open spaces, roads, streets, parks, pleasure or recreation grounds, or for the purpose of executing any work upon or under the land incidental to a town planning scheme, whether in the nature of a building work or not, and the decision of the Minister [of Health] whether land is likely to be used for building purposes or not, shall be final and conclusive.

Hewart complained that provisions such as these conferred excessive and unchallengeable discretions on ministers (to be exercised, in practice, by officials), undermining the rule of law.

He had a point.

Suppose, hypothetically, that Parliament has enacted a scheme for the making of grants to persons suffering from disability, stipulating that decisions on eligibility shall be made by local officers responsible for social security, and shall not be challengeable in the courts. Mrs Smith, who lives in Durham, believes herself to be suffering from disability and applies to her local officer for a grant, giving the reasons for her belief that she is entitled. He refuses her application, giving no reasons. She presses to know why she has been refused. The officer replies that he considers her to be ineligible because (a) her disability is mental, not physical; (b) she has not suffered from her disability for long enough to qualify for a grant; and (c) her disability is not sufficiently severe. Mrs Smith, now advised by a solicitor or a Citizens' Advice Bureau, asks the officer for the grounds on which he excludes mental disability, what period is laid down as the qualifying period, and what is the standard of severity required for a grant. She points out that her sister, Mrs Brown, who lives in Newcastle, is in a very similar position to herself, and has received a grant. The officer replies, declining to answer Mrs Smith's questions but saying that the decision is one for him alone and he has decided she shall not receive a grant. As for her sister, Mrs Brown in Newcastle, the officer points out that he is not responsible for that area, and if the officer there takes a different view, so be it. In the absence of an effective means to challenge the Durham officer's decision, such a regime would plainly violate the rule of law. Mrs Smith's entitlement should be governed by law, not by the arbitrary whim of an official.

The principle does not of course apply only to grants by the state. We expect the taxes we pay to be governed by detailed statutory rules, not by the decision of our local tax inspector. He has the duty to apply the rules laid down, but cannot invent new rules of his own. Nor has he an unlimited power to remit taxes lawfully due: as one judge succinctly said: 'One should be taxed by law, and not be untaxed by discretion.'[2]

This does not mean that every decision affecting the rights or liabilities of the citizen should be made by a court or tribunal, or that the criteria governing administrative decisions should be prescribed in statute or regulations made under statute. In practice, countless decisions are made every day by administrators charged with the duty of running our complex society, as, for example, on the allocation of housing to the homeless, the allocation of school places, the granting of planning permission, the granting of leave to enter the country and so on. What matters is that decisions should be based on stated criteria and that they should be amenable to legal challenge, although a challenge is unlikely to succeed if the decision was one legally and reasonably open to the decision-maker.

Even if the general thrust of Dicey and Hewart's argument is accepted, there is danger in carrying it to the extreme, by holding that officials or ministers charged with making decisions affecting the rights or liabilities of the citizen should have no discretion at all. Such a degree of inflexibility built into the system would make no allowance for the exceptional case calling for special treatment, which would itself be a source of injustice. In the immigration field, for example, judges have frequently and gratefully invited the Secretary of State to exercise his discretion to grant leave to enter the country or remain here to applicants who do not meet the tests for entry laid down in the immigration rules but whose personal history or circumstances demand sympathetic consideration. In a case crying out for compassionate treatment, we would not wish the Secretary of State to be obliged to wring his hands and plead inability to intervene.

What is true of ministers and officials is, generally, true of judges. As was said by Lord Shaw of Dunfermline nearly a century ago, 'To remit the maintenance of constitutional right to the region of judicial discretion is to shift the foundations of freedom from the rock to the sand.'[3] Another senior judge more recently made a similar point: 'And if it comes to the forensic crunch ... it must be law, not discretion, which is in command.'[4] The job of judges is to apply the law, not to indulge their personal preferences. There are areas in which they are required to exercise a discretion, but such discretions are much more closely constrained than is always acknowledged.

In the ordinary course of their judicial lives, judges in civil cases are repeatedly called upon to make judgments which involve no exercise of discretion at all. Thus there may be a dispute whether commercial parties made a concluded contract, whether a testator was of sound mind when executing a will, whether an accident victim is likely to suffer epilepsy, whether a ship was seaworthy when it put to sea, whether a footpath had been regularly used by the public for years, whether an invention was novel, whether a tyre had burst immediately before a road accident, and so on and so on. In such cases the judge must decide what evidence to accept and what to reject, must assess the probabilities, must consider any documents and expert evidence that bear on the issue, and must then give his ruling. He must exercise a judgment, not a discretion. Having reached his judgment he has no more discretion than a historian has to decide that King John did not execute Magna Carta at Runnymede in June 1215, when all the evidence suggests that he did.

But some exercises of judicial power are usually described as discretionary. For example, while some remedies, notably damages, may be claimed as of right if liability and resulting damage are proved against a defendant, others, notably an injunction, are discretionary in the sense that the judge is not bound to grant an injunction even if liability is proved. He has a discretion whether to grant one or not.

But rules have grown up to direct the exercise of this discretion. If the defendant's conduct is shown to be unlawful, and to be likely to cause harm to the claimant for which he will not be adequately compensated by damages, and if the defendant appears likely to go on doing whatever it is that the claimant complains of and gives no undertaking to desist, the judge is virtually bound to grant an injunction restraining the defendant from acting in that way. He has a discretion, but it is a discretion in name only because it can only be exercised one way.

In statutes the word 'may' (as opposed to 'shall' or 'must') is ordinarily understood to confer a discretion: the judge (or the minister, or whoever) may do whatever it is, but is not bound to do so. Thus, while a judge in a criminal trial ordinarily has no discretion to refuse to allow evidence to be given which is admissible under the rules governing the admissibility of evidence, section 78(1) of the Police and Criminal Evidence Act 1984 creates a discretionary exception. The section says:

In any proceedings the court may refuse to allow evidence on which the prosecution proposes to rely to be given if it appears to the court that, having regard to all the circumstances, including the circumstances in which the evidence was obtained, the admission of the evidence would have such an adverse effect on the fairness of the proceedings that the court ought not to admit it.

The court 'may': therefore it has a discretion. But it is a discretion which may only be exercised if – a big if – it appears to the court that having regard to the matters mentioned the admission of the evidence would have such an adverse effect on the fairness of the proceedings that the court ought not to admit it (as might be so, for example, if it were shown that a witness had been tricked or bribed into giving a statement). Whether or not it so appears to the court calls for an exercise of judgment, but not an exercise of discretion. It either does or does not appear to the court. If it does not, the court has no power to refuse to allow the evidence to be given (just as it has no power to refuse to allow admissible evidence to be given on which the defence proposes to rely). But if it does appear to the court that the admission of the evidence would have such an adverse effect on the fairness of the proceedings that the court ought not to admit it, the discretion can only properly be exercised in favour of excluding it. As in the case of many judicial discretions, a prior judgment must be made which effectively determines how the discretion should be exercised.

The awarding of costs in a civil action in the UK is always said to be in the discretion of the judge. But again it is not a free-ranging discretion. The ordinary rule is that the loser of the action is ordered to pay the reasonable costs incurred by the winner in winning it. Thus an unsuccessful claimant usually pays the defendant's costs: he should not have brought the action. An unsuccessful defendant usually pays the claimant's costs: he should have paid what was due and not defended the action. Not infrequently, the honours of war are shared, and neither side is the clear winner. Then the judge must apportion the costs so as to reflect the parties' respective degrees of success and failure, and may conclude that no order should be made. Exceptionally, a winning party may be denied his costs and, much more often, a losing party without means may escape an order to pay them. But the broad principles to be applied are clear. There is very little room for arbitrariness.

It is widely (and rightly) regarded as important that judges should enjoy a measure of discretion when passing sentence on convicted criminals, since if they are obliged to impose a prescribed penalty for a given offence they are unable to take account of the difference between one offence and another and between one offender and another. This makes for injustice, since offences vary widely in gravity, even with offences of the same description, and the circumstances of individual offenders are almost infinitely various. Parliament generally recognizes the value of such a discretion, and usually lays down a maximum penalty but only rarely a fixed or minimum penalty. It is also, however, a source of injustice if the severity of a criminal sentence is dictated by judicial prejudice or predilection, or whimsy (as in a case reported a number of years ago when a judge told a defendant convicted of a reasonably serious crime that he would ordinarily send him to prison, but would not because it was the judge's birthday). It would also be unjust if the severity of sentencing varied unduly in different parts of the country, a sentencing postcode lottery.

Current arrangements generally preserve the judge's sentencing discretion, but constrain it in three ways. First, sentencing guidelines and decisions are promulgated which indicate the appropriate range of sentence for different offences, identifying factors which may aggravate or mitigate the offence. Secondly, a defendant sentenced in the Crown Court can seek to appeal against his sentence, and if the Court of Appeal considers the sentence significantly too severe on the particular facts in the light of the guidelines and earlier decisions it will reduce it to an appropriate level. Thirdly, the Attorney General can seek leave to refer a sentence to the Court of Appeal as unduly lenient. Occasional cases had arisen in which public opinion was, rightly, outraged by the inadequacy of sentences passed on convicted defendants, against which the prosecution could not appeal, and this relatively new power was introduced to allow the Court of Appeal, at the instance of the Attorney General, to increase an unduly lenient sentence to an appropriate level. But public and political comment are not a sure guide. Some will recall the public outcry and criticism by the Home Secretary of a sentence imposed in June 2006 on a child kidnapper and abuser named Craig Sweeney. The Attorney General considered the Home Secretary's intervention unhelpful, and did not refer the sentence to the court as unduly lenient. The experienced judge who imposed the sentence had acted in loyal compliance with the scale laid down by the guidelines and earlier decisions.

The rule of law does not require that official or judicial decision-makers should be deprived of all discretion, but it does require that no discretion should be unconstrained so as to be potentially arbitrary. No discretion may be legally unfettered.

5

Equality Before the Law

(3) The laws of the land should apply equally to all, save to the extent that objective differences justify differentiation

In the first century AD St Paul rejected discrimination in terms breathtaking in their modernity: 'There is neither Jew nor Greek, there is neither bond nor free, there is neither male nor female: for ye are all one in Christ Jesus.'[1] His declaration was the more remarkable since he belonged to a society which accepted slavery, discriminated against women and gave special rights to Roman citizens. It was only his status as a Roman citizen which enabled him to protest at being punished before he had been tried, and entitled him to appeal to Caesar in Rome: 'Hast thou appealed unto Caesar?' asked Festus. 'Unto Caesar thou shalt go.'[2]

Most British people today would, I think, rightly regard equality before the law as a cornerstone of our society. There should not be one law for the rich and another for the poor. We would recognize the truth of what Thomas Rainborough, a Cromwellian colonel, famously said in 1647 in the army debates at Putney: 'For really I think, the poorest he that is in England has a life to live as the greatest he.'[3] But we would also accept that some categories of people should be treated differently because their position is in some important respect different. Children are the most obvious example. Children are, by definition, less mature than a normal adult, and should not therefore be treated as a normal adult would expect to be treated. Thus they are not liable to be prosecuted for crime below a certain age (in Britain it is conclusively presumed that no child under the age of ten can be guilty of any offence, a younger age than in most comparable European countries); if convicted of crime, they should not be punished as a normal adult would be punished; and they enjoy certain advantages in civil litigation. The mentally ill are another example: they may have to be confined if they present a danger to themselves or others. Prisoners, too, are treated differently from the rest of the population, since the very object of imprisonment is to curtail rights (notably, personal liberty) which are enjoyed by the rest of the population. Those who have no right of abode in this country are necessarily treated differently for immigration purposes from citizens who have a right of abode, since those without the right need leave to enter or remain in the country, which citizens do not. None of these examples (which could of course be multiplied) is problematical, so long as the law treats people differently because their positions are, genuinely, different. But any departure from the general rule of equal treatment should be scrutinized to ensure that the differential treatment is based on real differences. Otherwise, principle (3) is infringed.

The general principle that all should be equal before the law may now be accepted without much question, but it has taken time to reach that position. Not until 1772, for instance, did the English common law set its face against slavery in Britain. In that year the great case of James Somerset (or Sommersett – it is not at all clear how he spelled his name) was decided.[4] Somerset was born in Africa but taken to Virginia, where he was bought by one Stewart, who, after a sojourn in Massachusetts, brought him to London.[5] There he absconded and, although recaptured, refused to return to Stewart's service. Stewart accordingly sent him by force to a vessel bound for Jamaica, there to be held in irons until the ship sailed. The anti-slavery lobby in London, which had been anxiously awaiting a suitable test case, chose this. A writ of habeas corpus was issued, directed to the captain of the vessel, and a long series of hearings followed before Lord Mansfield, the Lord Chief Justice. It is an oddity of the case that the aphorism most closely associated with it – that 'the air of England is too pure for a slave to breathe' – appeared not in the judgment of Lord Mansfield but in the submissions of counsel[6] who borrowed it from a surprising source, a judgment of the Court of Star Chamber.[7] It is also an oddity of the case that Lord Mansfield's judgment did not conclude, as Lord Denning later claimed,[8] with the ringing declaration

'Let the black go free' but with the somewhat less resonant conclusion 'and therefore the black must be discharged'.[9] The decision meant freedom for Somerset, and was a triumph for the abolitionists. There were no longer, in Britain, to be bond and free. But the *Oxford Dictionary of National Biography*, perhaps rather sadly, records of Somerset: 'When he stepped out of Westminster Hall in July 1772 [after Lord Mansfield's judgment in his favour] he also stepped out of the historical record. Nothing is known, as yet, of his life (or death) and he remains very much a shadow at the centre of events controlled by others.'[10]

So one battle, a very important battle, had been won, but the war continued, and it is a regrettable fact that British law not only tolerated but imposed disabilities on Roman Catholics, Dissenters and Jews not rationally based on their religious beliefs, and disabilities on women not rationally connected with any aspect of their gender. Not until 1928 did women achieve full voting rights in this country.[11] Britain was not alone in tolerating inequality. The revolutionary French Declaration of the Rights of Man and the Citizen, universal in its scope, was amended to deny rights to certain categories of people. The Bill of Rights adopted by the United States, while progressive and ground-breaking in many ways, did not disturb the peculiar institution of slavery cherished in the South, which endured for ninety years after *Somerset's case*. No one needs to be reminded of the discrimination sanctioned by law against Jews, homosexuals and Gypsies in some European countries during the twentieth century.

It would be comforting to treat principle (3) as of antiquarian interest only. But this would be unrealistic, as the treatment of non-nationals in Britain and elsewhere reveals. As already pointed out, the position of a non-national with no right of abode in Britain differs from that of a national with a right of abode in the obvious and important respect that the one is subject to removal and the other is not. That is the crucial distinction, and differentiation relevant to it is unobjectionable and indeed inevitable. But it does not warrant differentiation irrelevant to that distinction, as Lord Scarman made clear in a House of Lords case in 1983:

Habeas corpus protection is often expressed as limited to 'British subjects'. Is it really limited to British nationals? Suffice it to say that the case law has given an emphatic 'no' to the question. Every person within the jurisdiction enjoys the equal protection of our laws. There is no distinction between British nationals and others. He who is subject to English law is entitled to its protection. This principle has been in the law at least since Lord Mansfield freed 'the black' in *Sommersett's Case* (1772) 20 St T 1.[12]

The message seems clear enough. But it did not deter Parliament from providing, in Part 4 of the Anti-terrorism, Crime and Security Act 2001, for the indefinite detention without charge or trial of non-nationals suspected of international terrorism, while exempting from that liability British nationals who were judged qualitatively to present the same risk at the time. This provision was held by the House of Lords to be incompatible with the European Convention on Human Rights,[13] and the terrorist attacks in London in July 2005 were carried out by British citizens and not foreign nationals. The Government, however, considered that it would be 'a very grave step' to detain British citizens in a similar way and that 'such draconian powers would be difficult to justify', prompting a joint parliamentary committee to observe that the Government's explanation appeared to suggest 'that it regards the liberty interests of foreign nationals as less worthy of protection than exactly the same interests of UK nationals'.[14]

But it would be wrong to regard the UK as the only, or the worst, offender in this regard. As an American academic author has written (see Chapter 11 below) with reference to the United States, 'Virtually every significant government security initiative implicating civil liberties – including penalizing speech, ethnic profiling, guilt by association, the use of administrative measures to avoid the safeguards of the criminal process, and preventive detention – has originated in a measure targeted at noncitizens.'[15] There is, I think, profound truth in the observation of a great American judge, Justice Jackson, in the Supreme Court of the United States in 1949:

I regard it as a salutary doctrine that cities, states and the Federal Government must exercise their powers so as not to discriminate between their inhabitants except upon some reasonable differentiation fairly related to the object of regulation. This equality is not merely abstract justice. The framers of the Constitution knew, and we should not forget today, that there is no more effective practical guaranty against arbitrary and unreasonable government than to require that the principles of law which officials would impose upon a minority must be imposed generally. Conversely, nothing opens the door to arbitrary action so effectively as to allow those officials to pick and choose only a few to whom they will apply legislation and thus to escape the political retribution that might be visited upon them if larger numbers were affected. Courts can take no better measure to assure that laws will be just than to require that laws be equal in operation.[16]

Sixty years on, we may say 'amen' to that. We may add that the rule of law requires no less.

6

The Exercise of Power

(4) Ministers and public officers at all levels must exercise the powers conferred on them in good faith, fairly, for the purpose for which the powers were conferred, without exceeding the limits of such powers and not unreasonably

This principle follows naturally from the two principles just considered, and indeed may be said to be inherent in them. But it deserves separate mention, since many would regard it as lying at the very heart of the rule of law principle. It is indeed fundamental. For although the citizens of a democracy empower their representative institutions to make laws which, duly made, bind all to whom they apply, and it falls to the executive, the government of the day and its servants, to carry these laws into effect, nothing ordinarily authorizes the executive to act otherwise than in strict accordance with those laws.

The process by which the courts enforce compliance by public authorities with the law has come to be known as judicial review. David Blunkett (Home Secretary from 2001 to 2004) has said that 'Judicial review is a modern invention. It has been substantially in being from the early 1980s . . .'.[1] He is right that powers of judicial review have been exercised much more extensively over the past thirty to forty years than they were before. But they are old powers, exercised for centuries. Hence the Latin names by which the remedies were traditionally known: habeas corpus, certiorari, mandamus, quo warranto, and so on, none of which has a very late twentieth-century ring to it. Habeas corpus and certiorari we have already encountered. By an order of mandamus the court orders a person, corporation, minister or tribunal to perform a legal obligation. A writ of quo warranto enquired by what warrant or authority a person exercised a particular right.

'Judicial review' is an excellent description of this exercise because it emphasizes that the judges are reviewing the lawfulness of administrative action taken by others. This is an appropriate judicial function, since the law is the judges' stock-in-trade, the field in which they are professionally expert. But they are not independent decision-makers, and have no business to act as such. They have, in all probability, no expertise in the subject matter of the decision they are reviewing. They are auditors of legality: no more, but no less.

This is important. When Parliament, by statute or statutory regulations, empowers a specific officer (such as a secretary of state, or the Director of Public Prosecutions or the Director of the Serious Fraud Office) or a specific body (such as a housing authority, a social services department, a county council, a health authority, a harbour board or the managers of a mental hospital) to make a particular decision, it does not empower anyone else. It expects that officer or body to follow any guidelines on policy that may have been laid down, but expects that the officer or body will exercise his or its own judgment, having regard to any relevant experience and the availability of resources. It does not expect, or intend, that the decision should be made by some judge who may think that he or she knows better. But there is a presumption that the decision made will be in accordance with the law. It is what lawyers call an irrebuttable presumption: one that is conclusive and cannot be trumped.

As would be expected, rules have developed to identify the kinds of unlawfulness which will lead to a successful application for judicial review, although even then the role of the court is ordinarily to quash the existing decision and order the nominated decision-maker to make another, lawful, decision; or to restrain the decision-maker from doing something which is proposed but would be unlawful if done; or to order the decision-maker to do something which the decision-maker is legally bound to do but is failing to do.

The kinds of unlawfulness which will found a successful application for judicial review have been described in somewhat different terms by different commentators and authorities, but those included in this principle provide a workable checklist. First is the requirement that statutory powers should be exercised in good faith – that is, honestly. It is presumed that Parliament intends no less. It has indeed been described as the first principle of judicial review that a discretion must be exercised in good faith.[2] Cases in which bad faith is established are rare, but in one case in 1991 a Court of Appeal judge found that '[this] decision-making ... can only in the circumstances have been activated in my view by bad faith or, in a word, vindictiveness. It was thus an abuse of power contrary to the public good.'[3]

A power must also be exercised in a way that, in all the circumstances, is fair, since it is assumed (in the absence of a clearly expressed contrary intention) that the state does not intend to treat the citizen unfairly. It may of course be a vexed question what, in the particular circumstances, fairness requires. But the so-called rules of natural justice have traditionally been held to demand, first, that the mind of the decision-maker should not be tainted by bias or personal interest (he must not be a judge in his own cause) and, secondly, that anyone who is liable to have an adverse decision made against him should have a right to be heard (a rule the venerability of which is vouched by its Latin version: audi alteram partem, hear the other party). This is a principle to which the courts tend to attach great importance, and it has been described as

the necessary assumption on which to base an argument ... that the court must supplement the procedural requirements which the Act itself stipulates by implying additional requirements said to be necessary to ensure that the principles of natural justice are observed ... The decided cases on this subject establish the principle that the courts will readily imply terms where necessary to ensure fairness of procedure for the protection of parties who may suffer a detriment in consequence of administrative action.[4]

In a case in which the Home Secretary had retrospectively increased the minimum term which a life sentence prisoner was to serve before consideration of parole, Lord Steyn (quoted in Chapter 1) said, in 1997: 'And the rule of law enforces minimum standards of fairness, both substantive and procedural.'[5]

A decision-making power conferred by statute must always be exercised so as to advance the policy and objects of the Act, and not to frustrate them or advance some other object. As has been said,

Parliament must have conferred the discretion with the intention that it should be used to promote the policy and objects of the Act; the policy and objects of the Act must be determined by construing the Act as a whole and construction is always a matter of law for the court. In a matter of this kind it is not possible to draw a hard and fast line, but if the Minister, by reason of his having misconstrued the Act or for any other reason, so uses his discretion as to thwart or run counter to the policy and objects of the Act, then our law would be very defective if persons aggrieved were not entitled to the protection of the court.[6]

This was said in a case in which the Minister of Agriculture, having power to appoint a committee to investigate complaints, had unaccountably refused to do so. The principle has also been expressed more snappily: 'Statutory power conferred for public purposes is conferred as it were upon trust, not absolutely – that is to say, it can validly be used only in the right and proper way which Parliament when conferring it is presumed to have intended.'[7] On some occasions, happily rare, statutory powers are exercised for an obviously improper purpose. A memorable example is the scheme by which the Westminster City Council in the late 1980s exercised a statutory power to sell council properties so as to replace council tenants by owner-occupiers in marginal wards on the ground that owner-occupiers would be more likely than council tenants to vote for the (Conservative) majority party. In that instance, the matter did not reach the court in time for it to quash the scheme or restrain its implementation. But the two leading members of the council were found to have wilfully misconducted themselves, and were ordered to make good the loss suffered by the council, in the sum of £31 million (only part of which was, in the event, paid).[8]

It is an elementary principle that anyone purporting to exercise a statutory power must not act beyond or outside the limits of the power conferred. Here again the principle is so old that it is often known by its Latin name: ultra vires, beyond the powers. It is common sense. If a head teacher has statutory authority to exclude a disruptive pupil for (say) two weeks, he or she cannot lawfully exclude a pupil for a month. If a local authority has statutory power to borrow up to £10 million, it cannot lawfully borrow £100 million. If hospital managers have statutory authority to detain compulsorily a patient suffering from severe mental illness, they cannot lawfully detain compulsorily a patient not so suffering. There would be little or no point in laying down legal limits if they could be broken without legal consequence. In one case it was held that an order would be ultra vires if purporting to permit a criminal offence because 'Parliament is assumed not to have intended that statutory powers should be used to facilitate the commission of criminal offences'.[9]

Unreasonableness is more difficult territory, since a judge invited to quash a decision as unreasonable may be tempted to consider what he would have decided had he been the decision-maker, and to find the decision unreasonable because he would have reached a different decision. The test is sometimes described as one of irrationality, and this is perhaps a preferable usage since it emphasizes that the threshold of judicial interference on this ground is, as it should be, a high one. Some vivid expressions have been used to show how high: in one case a Law Lord referred to a need to show that the consequences of the Secretary of State's guidance 'were so absurd that he must have taken leave of his senses',[10] but in later cases this test tends to be cited only by judges who are ruling that the decision under challenge was not unreasonable or irrational. A more orthodox, and better, test is whether the conduct which it is sought to challenge was 'conduct which no sensible authority acting with due appreciation of its responsibilities would have decided to adopt'.[11] But even that test must be applied with caution since, as has been correctly held, 'Two reasonable [persons] can perfectly reasonably come to opposite conclusions on the same set of facts without forfeiting their title to be regarded as reasonable ... Not every reasonable exercise of judgment is right, and not every mistaken exercise of judgment is unreasonable. There is a band of decisions within which no court should seek to replace the individual's judgment with his own.'[12] It is often sufficient to ask whether the challenged decision was 'within the range of reasonable decisions open to a decision maker'.[13] Decisions have, however, been held to be unreasonable if, for example, they were illogical or inconsistent with another decision.[14]

If the judges were themselves to exercise powers which properly belong elsewhere it would be a usurpation of authority and they would themselves be acting unlawfully. As Lord Hailsham pointed out in his 1983 Hamlyn Lectures, Thomas Fuller's warning quoted in Chapter 1 ('Be you never so high, the Law is above you') applies to judges no less than ministers.[15] But in properly exercising judicial power to hold ministers, officials and public bodies to account the judges usurp no authority. They exercise a constitutional power which the rule of law requires that they should exercise. This does not of course endear them to those whose decisions are successfully challenged. Least of all does it endear them when the decision is a high-profile decision of moment to the government of the day, whatever its political colour. Governments have no more appetite for losing cases than anyone else, perhaps even less, since they believe themselves to be acting in the public interest and, in addition to the expense and disappointment of losing, they may be exposed to the taunts of their political opponents (who might, if in office, have done just the same). This is the inescapable consequence of living in a state governed by the rule of law. There are countries in the world where all judicial decisions find favour with the powers that be, but they are probably not places where any of us would wish to live.

7

Human Rights

(5) The law must afford adequate protection of fundamental human rights

This is not a principle which would be universally accepted as embraced within the rule of law. Dicey, it has been argued, gave no such substantive content to his rule of law concept.[1] Professor Raz has written:

A non-democratic legal system, based on the denial of human rights, on extensive poverty, on racial segregation, sexual inequalities, and religious persecution may, in principle, conform to the requirements of the rule of law better than any of the legal systems of the more enlightened Western democracies . . . It will be an immeasurably worse legal system, but it will excel in one respect: in its conformity to the rule of law . . . The law may . . . institute slavery without violating the rule of law.[2]

This is close to what some economists have called a 'thin' definition of the rule of law.[3] On the other hand, as Geoffrey Marshall has pointed out, chapters V to XII of Dicey's great work, in which he discusses what would now be called civil liberties, appear within Part II of the book, entitled 'The Rule of Law'. As Marshall observes, 'the reader could be forgiven for thinking that Dicey intended them to form part of what the rule of law meant for Englishmen'.[4] Both the Universal Declaration of Human Rights and later international instruments link the protection of human rights with the rule of law, and the European Court of Human Rights has referred to 'the notion of the rule of law from which the whole Convention draws its inspiration'.[5] The

European Commission has consistently treated democratization, the rule of law, respect for human rights and good governance as insepa-rably interlinked.[6]

While, therefore, one can recognize the logical force of Professor Raz's contention, I would roundly reject it in favour of a 'thick' defi-nition, embracing the protection of human rights within its scope. A state which savagely represses or persecutes sections of its people cannot in my view be regarded as observing the rule of law, even if the transport of the persecuted minority to the concentration camp or the compulsory exposure of female children on the mountainside is the subject of detailed laws duly enacted and scrupulously observed. So to hold would, I think, be to strip 'the existing constitutional prin-ciple of the rule of law' affirmed by section 1 of the Constitutional Reform Act 2005 and widely recognized in the laws of other countries around the world, of much of its virtue. This was accepted by the President of the Constitutional Court of the Russian Federation (V. D. Zorkin) at a symposium held by the International Bar Association in Moscow on 6 July 2007, when, as part of a lecture on the morality of law, he said:

Steps such as adoption of liberal laws, acknowledgement of common prin-ciples and norms of international law, and creation of corresponding state and public institutions are insufficient for the real rule of law. It is also important that statutes express the essence of law as mankind understands it at each particular stage of its development. The great philosopher Spinoza once said that law was the mathematics of freedom.

Law cannot be simply what is dictated by political authority or issued by the state. In the 20th Century there have been two examples of legal trag-edies which were developing in parallel. One was totalitarian Soviet Com-munism, and the other German Nazism. In the USSR, owing to efforts of the Stalinist regime theoretician Vyshinsky, the law was identified with stat-utory law, and law was identified with the will (or rather dictatorship) of the proletariat. Through such logic, whatever was prescribed by the state in the form of statutory law was lawful.

Hitler followed yet a different ideological pathway, absolutely antagonis-tic to communist ideology, but the result was the same. In Nazi Germany, the law was an expression of the will of the German nation, and the will of the German nation was incorporated in the Führer. Hence the law existed only as a body of statutory laws.

Both systems were killing millions of people, because for both the law was given and contained in the statutes.

It is, of course, for states to decide what rights they will protect by law, and what sanctions they will impose for breach.

But this is a difficult area since there is no universal consensus on the rights and freedoms which are fundamental, even among civilized nations. In some developing countries a higher premium is put on economic growth than on protection of individual rights, and in some Islamic countries little or no protection is given to some rights which are cherished elsewhere. It must be accepted that the outer edges of some fundamental human rights are not clear-cut. But within a given society there is ordinarily a large measure of agreement on where the lines are to be drawn at any particular time, even though standards change over time, and in the last resort the courts are there to draw them. It is, I think, possible to identify the rights and freedoms which, in the UK and developed Western or Westernized countries elsewhere, are seen as fundamental, and the rule of law requires that those rights should be protected.

I cannot, within the reasonable confines of a chapter such as this, attempt to describe other than superficially the protection afforded to fundamental human rights in this country today. But I shall briefly review the rights which most regularly feature in discussion and court decisions, suggesting a number of conclusions: that the common law and statute have for many years given a measure of protection to such rights; that there were gaps in such protection; that the rights and freedoms embodied in the European Convention on Human Rights, given direct effect in this country by the Human Rights Act 1998, are in truth 'fundamental', in the sense that they are guarantees which no one living in a free democratic society such as the UK should be required to forgo; and that protection of these rights does not, as is sometimes suggested, elevate the rights of the individual over the rights of the community to which he belongs. The Convention rights scheduled to the Human Rights Act provide a convenient framework for my review.

Article 2: The right to life

This article provides that 'Everyone's right to life shall be protected by law' and tightly restricts the circumstances in which life may lawfully be taken (as, for example, where taking life is absolutely necessary to defend another person from unlawful violence). The exceptions do not now include the taking of life by the state in execution of a sentence imposed following conviction of crime. The right to life has been described as the most fundamental of all rights,[7] and it is indeed obvious that unless a person is alive he or she can enjoy no other rights.

As would be expected, English law has long protected this important right by (in particular) criminalizing murder, manslaughter, infanticide and causing death by dangerous driving, by having no truck with euthanasia and by imposing civil liability on those who cause death negligently but not criminally. Suicide has not since 1961 been a crime, but it is still a crime to help someone else to take or attempt to take his own life. This accords with what the European Court of Human Rights, interpreting Article 2, has held to be a substantive obligation on member states not to take life without justification. But it has gone further, and interpreted Article 2 as imposing a substantive obligation to establish a framework of laws, precautions, procedures and means of enforcement which will, to the greatest extent reasonably practicable, protect life.[8] And it has gone still further, interpreting Article 2 as imposing on member states a procedural obligation to supplement these substantive obligations: to initiate an effective public investigation by an independent official body into any death occurring in circumstances in which it appears that one or other of the foregoing substantive obligations has, or may have been, violated, and it appears that agents of the state may be implicated.[9] Thus when a young Asian detainee was battered to death at Feltham Young Offenders' Institution by a rabidly racist cellmate on 21 March 2000, the House of Lords in October 2003 ordered that a public inquiry be held into the circumstances of the killing,[10] an order which would have been most improbable but for the Human Rights Act.

Article 2 is invoked where a death has occurred, and it cannot therefore afford redress to the deceased. But the family and close relatives of the deceased are rightly regarded as victims: they have a legitimate interest in finding out what happened, and may derive some comfort from knowing that lessons have been learned which may prevent repetition. There is nothing here which elevates the rights of the victim over those of the community. The Convention's exception, where life is taken when absolutely necessary to defend a person from unlawful violence, chimes with the wider common law rule which sanctions the use of force to defend person or property, provided the force used is reasonable on the facts as the killer believes them to be. The common law does not leave the victim defenceless, but nor does it sanction the taking of life where such a degree of violence is unreasonable.

Article 3: The prohibition of torture

Article 3 of the Convention provides that 'No one shall be subjected to torture or to inhuman or degrading treatment or punishment.' As explained in Chapter 2, the common law (followed by statute) set its face against torture several centuries ago and the Bill of Rights 1689 forbade the infliction of cruel and unusual punishments. Most forms of violence to the person have been criminally punishable or civilly actionable, or both, for a very long time. There is no doubting the importance which most people would attach to protection against what the Convention forbids.

Times, however, change. In 1993 the Judicial Committee of the Privy Council, hearing an appeal from Jamaica in a case where the death penalty had been lawfully imposed, had to consider whether it was cruel and unusual punishment (the language used in Article 17(2) of the Jamaican Constitution) to execute the defendant after he had spent an excessive period on death row following sentence and awaiting execution. It held (departing from an earlier decision) that it was.[11] In a case brought by Ireland against the UK complaining of the treatment to which nationalist suspects had been subjected in Northern Ireland, the European Court of Human Rights held that the treatment complained of, although inhuman or degrading, fell short of torture,[12] but it may well be that on the same facts a different ruling would now be given. In a later case the European Court held that

> having regard to the fact that the Convention is a 'living instrument which must be interpreted in the light of present-day conditions' ... certain acts which were classified in the past as 'inhuman and degrading treatment' as opposed to 'torture' could be classified differently in future ... the increasingly high standard being required in the area of the protection of human rights and fundamental liberties correspondingly and inevitably requires greater firmness in assessing breaches of the fundamental values of democratic societies.[13]

In a Scottish case, the conditions in Barlinnie Prison in Glasgow were held to be so bad as to violate Article 3.[14] It is clear that Article 3 has extended the reach of the common law.

Article 4: Prohibition of slavery and forced labour

Article 4 provides that 'No one shall be held in slavery or servitude'. It also provides that 'No one shall be forced to perform forced or compulsory labour', although this provision is subject to some exclusions (work in prisons, compulsory military service or a non-military alternative, service exacted to meet a very grave emergency, performance of normal civic obligations).

This adds little or nothing to English common law and statute. It prohibits slavery, but also forbids forced labour of the kind which became familiar in some parts of Europe in the twentieth century. This again is a protection which no rational person would willingly forgo, and the exclusions recognize the needs of the community as a whole.

Article 5: Right to liberty and security

Article 5 is important, and has been invoked in many cases. It opens by declaring that 'Everyone has the right to liberty and security of person.' It then continues by providing that 'No one shall be deprived of his liberty save in the following cases and in accordance with a procedure prescribed by law.' Those cases relate to detention by court order following conviction; detention following breach of a court order; detention for the purpose of bringing a criminal suspect before a court or preventing him committing further offences or fleeing after doing so; detention of a minor for educational purposes or to bring him before a competent authority; detention of persons of unsound mind, alcoholics or drug addicts, vagrants, and people afflicted by infectious diseases; or detention to prevent illegal entry into the country or pending deportation or extradition. A person may not be detained unless his case falls within one or other of these categories.

This central provision is reinforced by a number of supplementary provisions. A person arrested must be told in a language he can understand why he has been arrested and of any charge against him. He shall be brought promptly before a court and is entitled to trial within a reasonable time or to release pending trial, perhaps on bail. A person detained may bring proceedings by which the lawfulness of his detention can be speedily decided and his release ordered if it is unlawful. Anyone detained in violation of the article must be compensated.

A few years ago Lord Donaldson of Lymington, the Master of the Rolls, observed that 'We have all been brought up to believe, and do believe, that the liberty of the citizen under the law is the most fundamental of all freedoms.'[15] This is no less than the truth, as the history of Magna Carta, habeas corpus, the Petition of Right and the Glorious Revolution and the story of James Somerset make clear. For centuries British citizens believed, not without reason, that personal liberty was protected in Britain as nowhere else on earth. It was protected of course by habeas corpus, but also by other processes of judicial review and by recognizing unjustified imprisonment as both a crime and an actionable civil wrong. The permissible grounds of detention summarized above largely follow the common law and may well have been inspired by British negotiators.

There can, however, be no denying that the Human Rights Act has, with the authority of Parliament (which required the courts and public authorities to comply with the Convention), empowered the courts to identify and make public declarations concerning infringements of liberty for which, without the Act, they could have given no redress at all. One example concerns a group of terrorist suspects detained without charge or trial in what became known as the *Belmarsh* case.[16] Another concerns a group of terrorist suspects confined to their assigned flats subject to stringent conditions for eighteen hours each day.[17] In both those cases, there was found to be an unjustified deprivation of liberty. But it is always necessary to decide whether what is complained of amounts to a deprivation, and it has been held that if a police officer exercises statutory powers to stop, search and question a person for a short time that person is not deprived of his liberty.[18] When demonstrators in London in 2001 were corralled by police at Oxford Circus for a number of hours, there was a difference of judicial and professional opinion whether they had been deprived of their liberty, the House of Lords holding that they had not.[19]

There are doubtless those who would wish to lock up all those suspected of terrorist and other serious offences and, in the time-honoured phrase, throw away the key. But a suspect is by definition a person against whom no offence has been proved. Suspicions, even if reasonably entertained, may prove to be misplaced, as a series of tragic miscarriages of justice has demonstrated. Police officers and security officials can be wrong. It is a gross injustice to deprive of his liberty for significant periods a person who has committed no crime and does not intend to do so. No civilized country should willingly tolerate such injustices.

Article 6: Right to a fair trial

The importance of this article for the rule of law is so central as to call for a principle of its own: see Chapter 9 below.

Article 7: No punishment without law

This article provides that 'No one shall be held guilty of any criminal offence on account of any act or omission which did not constitute a criminal offence under national or international law at the time when it was committed. Nor shall a heavier penalty be imposed than the one that was applicable at the time the criminal offence was committed.' There is a saving provision, perhaps intended to cover the Nuremberg trial of leading Nazis, for acts and omissions which at the time of their occurrence were criminal according to the general principles of law recognized by civilized nations.

This is a rule of simple fairness, a rule which any child would understand, and it has featured in most legal systems since Roman times. It has long featured in British law, although it has not been consistently observed: a statute in the time of Henry VIII[20] ordered that the Bishop of Rochester's cook, one Richard Rose, be boiled to death (he had put poison into the porridge in the Bishop's kitchen). But that was a long time ago. Difficult questions can sometimes arise on the retrospective effect of new statutes, but on this point the law is and has long been clear: you cannot be punished for something which was not criminal when you did it, and you cannot be punished more severely than you could have been punished at the time of the offence.

Article 8: Right to respect for private and family life

Article 8 of the European Convention differs from all other articles in one respect and from the articles so far considered in another.

It differs from all other articles in guaranteeing not a right to a particular outcome (life, freedom, a fair trial and so on) but a right to respect. Article 8(1) says that 'Everyone has the right to respect for his private and family life, his home and his correspondence.' This recognizes that there are important areas of our private and personal lives which we are entitled to keep to ourselves and into which, generally speaking, the state has no business to intrude.

This right to respect in Article 8(1), however, is qualified by what may be called a community exception, a recognition that the rights of the individual may properly be restricted, in the interests of the community at large, if certain fairly demanding conditions are satisfied. This community exception, somewhat differently expressed but to very much the same effect, also applies to Articles 9, 10 and 11. In Article 8(2) the community exception, as I call it, provides:

There shall be no interference by a public authority with the exercise of this right except such as is in accordance with the law and is necessary in a democratic society in the interests of national security, public safety or the economic well-being of the country, for the prevention of disorder or crime, for the protection of health or morals, or for the protection of the rights and freedoms of others.

Thus it is accepted that the rights of the individual may have to be curtailed for the benefit of the wider community, but only if three conditions are met: the interference must be in accordance with the law (other articles say 'prescribed by law', which better conveys the sense); the interference must be directed to one of the specified purposes; and it must be not merely desirable, useful or reasonable[21] but necessary in a democratic society and proportionate.

The protection given by the common law in this area has been patchy. It criminalized and gave civil remedies for assault (widely defined) and any violation of a person's bodily integrity. Historically, it was robust in asserting the inviolability of a person's home. Thus Sir Edward Coke, perhaps the most influential English jurist of all time, famously declared that 'a man's house is his castle',[22] and the Earl of Chatham scarcely less famously said:

The poorest man may in his cottage bid defiance to all the forces of the Crown. It may be frail – its roof may shake – the wind may blow through it – the storm may enter – the rain may enter – but the King of England cannot enter – all his forces dare not cross the threshold of the ruined tenement![23]

But that was also a long time ago. A recent pamphlet, *Crossing the Threshold*,[24] discusses '266 ways the State can enter your home' (and this now appears – see Chapter 11 – to be a considerable underestimate). All these grounds of entry have received the blessing of Parliament, and may be justified for one or another of the purposes recognized by the Convention, but it is plain that an Englishman's house is now a great deal more porous than Coke and Chatham ever conceived. There is no British law giving the protection afforded by the Fourth Amendment to the US Constitution (quoted in Chapter 2 above), which provides that 'The right of the people to be secure in their persons, houses, papers and effects, against unreasonable searches and seizures, shall not be violated . . .'. The common law was power-less to prevent the unregulated interception by the state of private telephone conversations until an adverse decision of the European Court compelled the government to legislate.[25] The common law also developed no coherent rules to protect privacy,[26] while protecting duties of confidence and, for instance, the privacy of a prisoner's cor-respondence with his legal advisers.[27]

The common law was not very sensitive to the claims of personal autonomy and, as the cases decided under the Convention demonstrate, this is a difficult area. While the core of the right to which Article 8 is directed is clear enough, the outer reaches of the protection are more nebulous. The European Court has understood 'private life' as extend-ing to those features which are integral to a person's identity or ability to function socially as a person,[28] but the drawing of lines to distin-guish an intrusion which is a violation of Article 8 from one which, however unwelcome, is no violation involves a difficult exercise of judgment. Difficult this area may be; unimportant it is not. As the material gathered about the public by government agencies multiplies exponentially (see Chapter 11 below), the need to decide when the legitimate interest of government becomes the intrusive surveillance of Big Brother seems likely to become ever more pressing.

Article 9: Freedom of thought, conscience and religion

Article 9(1) enshrines a fundamental value of a modern pluralist soci-ety. It provides that 'Everyone has the right to freedom of thought, conscience and religion; this right includes freedom to change his reli-gion or belief and freedom, either alone or in community with others and in public or private, to manifest his religion or belief, in worship, teaching, practice and observance.' By Article 8(2), freedom to manifest one's religion or beliefs is subject to a community exception similar to that already noticed. Thus you may believe what you like provided you keep your beliefs to yourself or share them with like-minded people, but when you put your beliefs into practice in a way that impinges on others, limits may be imposed, if prescribed by law, necessary in a democratic society and directed to one of the specified purposes.

While the principle is now (after a chequered history) regarded in Western countries as fundamental, the community qualification is scarcely less so, for within any society there will be some practices which will be regarded as beyond the pale of acceptance. If the adherents of different religions choose, for religious reasons, to abjure alcohol, or abstain from eating meat, these manifestations do not impinge on the interests of society as a whole. But a society such as ours could not countenance human sacrifice, or the self-immolation of widows on their husbands' funeral pyres, or female genital mutilation, however strongly those practices might be valued by those who follow other religions and traditions. In many countries of the world a man may lawfully have several wives, but not here: one, at a time, is enough.

These, it may fairly be said, are easy examples. The problems inevitably arise in borderline cases. Should Sikhs, whose religion requires the wearing of a comb in uncut hair (with which the wearing of a turban is closely associated), be exempt from the requirement, binding on others, to wear crash helmets when riding motorcycles or hard hats when working on building sites? The answer given is 'yes'.[29] Should Rastafarians have their dreadlocks cut off, as others have their hair cut, on admission to prison, or be exempt from the ordinary prohibitions on the use of cannabis? The answer to both questions is 'no'. Prison governors have been instructed to allow Rastafarian prisoners to keep their dreadlocks if they wish to do so, but the drugs law applies to them as to others.[30] Could the state prohibit the use of corporal punishment in schools in the teeth of some parents' religious belief, founded on certain verses in the Old Testament, in the moral value of the practice? The House of Lords held that it could.[31] Was a school, largely attended by Muslim pupils, with a predominantly Muslim governing body, entitled to insist on compliance with a dress code, approved by the Muslim authorities, which precluded the wearing of a garment which one pupil wanted to wear? The House of Lords held that it was.[32] But problems about the wearing of religious emblems and clothing are likely to recur.

The rule of law requires that fundamental rights, such as that of free-dom of belief and practice, should be protected, but it does not require that they should be absolute. The rights of the individual must be set against the rights of others, and that calls for the drawing of lines.

Article 10: Freedom of expression

Since the publication of John Milton's *Areopagitica* in 1644 the importance of free speech has been understood, if – in Britain and elsewhere – very incompletely honoured. It is important for the reason which he gave: 'Though all the winds of doctrine were let loose to play upon the earth, so Truth be in the field, we do injuriously by licensing and prohibiting to misdoubt her strength. Let her and false-hood grapple; who ever knew Truth put to the worse, in a free and open encounter?' In a modern democracy where the ultimate deci-sions rest with the people, it is the more important that they should be fully informed and empowered to choose between conflicting opin-ions and alternative courses of action. The media, of course, have a crucial role to play. As has been said, 'The proper functioning of a modern participatory democracy requires that the media be free, active, professional and inquiring.'[33] So we cannot doubt the signifi-cance of Article 10(1), which opens with the declaration that 'Every-one has the right to freedom of expression'. Thus we have freedom to be ourselves (Article 8), freedom to think what we like (Article 9) and freedom to say and write what we like and to publicize our view by demonstrating (Article 10). Article 10(1) continues: 'This right shall include freedom to hold opinions and to receive and impart informa-tion and ideas without interference by public authority and regardless of frontiers. This Article shall not prevent States from requiring the licensing of broadcasting, television or cinema enterprises.' Milton's dream has come much closer to fruition than it did in the England of his day.

Article 10(2) contains a community exception, subject to the con-ditions already noted but with a somewhat longer list of specified objects: they include the interests of territorial integrity, protection of the reputation or rights of others, preventing disclosure of information received in confidence, and maintaining the authority and impartiality of the judiciary.

Until Article 10 was given direct effect in this country by the Human Rights Act there was no legal right to free expression in Britain (unlike the United States). This does not mean that public discourse in Britain was severely constrained. It means that in practice everyone was free to write and say whatever they wished, provided it was not forbidden. The right existed in the very considerable space not occupied by prohibitions, which applied to statements that were libellous or slanderous, or a dishonest disparagement of another's goods, or in contempt of court, or a breach of copyright, or were obscene, or seditious, or incited mutiny or the commission of crime, or disclosed official secrets.

The tendency of the decisions made by the European Court in Strasbourg has been to enlarge the freedom of expression previously enjoyed in Britain, in relation, for example, to contempt of court[34] and the damages recoverable on proof of libel.[35] In the eyes of many commentators, particularly those in the media, British libel laws are seen as too restrictive, and certainly the press does not enjoy the freedom to criticize public figures which now prevails in some other countries, notably the United States. The challenge is to afford the media the greatest freedom to investigate, report, inform and comment but with a reasonable measure of protection, not least of those who are in the public and political arena.

Article 11: Freedom of assembly and association

Article 11 is the corollary of the rights just considered. We have freedom to be ourselves, to think what we like, to say what we like and (under this Article) to choose the company we like: we can associate with anyone willing to associate with us. Thus Article 11(1) provides that 'Everyone has the right to freedom of peaceful assembly and to freedom of association with others, including the right to form and to join trade unions for the protection of his interests.' The right to join a trade union has been held to include the right not to do so.[36] It is a genuine choice. But here again we find, in Article 11(2), a community exception, with a new addition: 'This Article shall not prevent the imposition of lawful restrictions on the exercise of these rights by members of the armed forces, of the police or of the administration of the State.'

Here again the article goes far beyond the existing law in this country, which conferred no right of assembly or association as such but depended very largely on an absence of prohibitions. The right can, however, be recognized as an important one, for two reasons in particular. First, man is a social animal, and for very many people the living of a contented and fulfilled life depends on the company and support of others, which they should not therefore be denied the opportunity to seek. Secondly, freedom of both assembly and association has a democratic, political dimension, enabling individuals collectively to publicize and campaign for the causes they believe in more effectively than any of them could hope to do on their own. It is a feature of imprisonment that those detained are denied the freedom to choose their associates, and this is an intentional feature of their punishment. Suspects subject to control orders are similarly subject to very severe restrictions on whom they may meet, and who may visit them.[37] Of course there are occasions when this important freedom has to be curtailed, as (for instance) when a riot is in the offing. But none of us, I think, would choose to have our social relations governed by the state.

Article 12: Right to marry

Article 12 provides that 'Men and women of marriageable age have the right to marry and to found a family, according to the national laws governing the exercise of this right.' Thus states may regulate (as the UK does) the age and capacity required for a valid marriage, and lay down procedural rules to be followed, but there is otherwise no community exception to this right. While same-sex couples may in Britain enter into legally recognized civil partnerships, there is no right (as in some American states) to enter into same-sex marriages, and Article 12 has not so far been interpreted to require this.

The abuse at which this article is targeted is, plainly enough, the prohibition of marriage between those of different races and religions and the forced sterilization of those not meeting some state-ordained eugenic standard. It might seem unlikely that the right would be of practical significance in Britain today. But in a very recent group of cases it has been held that, as operated by the Home Office, a scheme requiring some immigrants to obtain a certificate of the Secretary of State before they could contract a civil marriage violated the article.[38] It was also held (and the Home Office accepted) that the scheme was discriminatory, but that takes us on to the next article included in the Act.

Article 14

Article 14 provides that 'The enjoyment of the rights and freedoms set forth in this Convention shall be secured without discrimination on any ground such as sex, race, colour, language, religion, political or other opinion, national or social origin, association with a national minority, property, birth or other status.'

Two points may be made about this article. The first is that it does not contain a free-standing prohibition of discrimination. You cannot validly complain that you have been the victim of discrimination on one or other of the stated grounds without more: you must go further and show that you have been the victim of prohibited discrimination in the context of your enjoyment of one or more of the rights and freedoms set forth in the Convention. You do not have to show that a Convention right or freedom has actually been violated, but you must show that the discrimination occurred within the area (or, in the language used in the cases, within the ambit) of some Convention article.

The second point to be made is that the reach of Article 14 is remarkably broad. The list of stated grounds is very comprehensive, and covers most of the grounds on which discrimination is likely to occur. But even this far-reaching list is not exhaustive: what is prohibited is discrimination 'on any ground such as', so other grounds are not excluded;[39] and the expression 'or other status' is obviously broad enough to include grounds which have not occurred to the draftsmen of the Convention. It has been interpreted to refer to 'a personal characteristic ... by which persons or groups of persons are distinguishable from each other'.⁴⁰ A person's professional status, employment status, military rank, place of residence and previous employment by the KGB have all been held to qualify.⁴¹

This article gives effect, in the wide area it covers, to the principle of equality before the law. It would not be tolerable if people's right to enjoyment of the rights and freedoms in the Convention could law-fully be reduced because they were female, or homosexual, or belonged to an unpopular race, or were black, or Jewish, or Gypsies, or spoke a minority language, or were communists or aristocrats or landown-ers. It is unpopular minorities whom charters and bills of rights exist to protect. In almost any society, the majority (which usually includes the rich and powerful) can look after itself.

The main articles in the body of the Convention have been supple-mented by a number of later protocols, to some of which the UK has given legal effect. Two of these call for brief mention.

The First Protocol. Article 1. Protection of property

This article has two paragraphs. The first provides: 'Every natural or legal person is entitled to the peaceful enjoyment of his possessions. No one shall be deprived of his possessions except in the public interest and subject to the conditions provided for by law and by the general principles of international law.' The second paragraph is a qualification: 'The preceding provisions shall not, however, in any way impair the right of a State to enforce such laws as it deems neces-sary to control the use of property in accordance with the general interest or to secure the payment of taxes or other contributions or penalties.'

The article does two things. First, it prohibits the arbitrary confis-cation of people's property or possessions without compensation. The treatment of white farmers in Zimbabwe would be the most obvious violation. But, secondly, the article recognizes that, in some situations, it may be necessary to override private property rights for the benefit of the community as a whole. It may be necessary for the state to acquire my farm in order to build a motorway or a new airport, but the need must be shown and I must be compensated. It may be necessary to control the way I use my land to prevent my factory polluting the atmosphere or the local river. It may be necessary to seize and sell some of my goods if I do not pay my income or council tax, or fail to comply with a judgment of the court. But all this must be done pursuant to law, as the rule of law requires.

The First Protocol. Article 2. Right to education

Article 2 of the First Protocol opens by declaring that 'No one shall be denied the right to education.' This does not mean that everyone has the right to demand to be educated at the institution of his choice in any subject he may elect. It means that everyone shall be guaranteed fair access to such education as his home state provides.[42] The article continues: 'In the exercise of any functions which it assumes in relation to education and to teaching, the State shall respect the right of parents to ensure such education and teaching in conformity with their own religious and philosophical convictions.' The decided cases here relate to such matters as compulsory sex education,[43] religious education[44] and corporal punishment.[45] The thrust of this article accords with what, for many years, has been the thrust of educational policy in the UK: that education up to a certain age should be compulsory; that access to the country's educational facilities should be open to all; and that the reasonable wishes of parents should so far as possible be respected.

Conclusion

The negotiation and adoption of the European Convention in 1950, hot on the heels of the Universal Declaration and soon after the ending of the Second World War, were not an accident of timing. The Convention was a response to the oppression and tyranny which had scarred the continent of Europe during a period when every right discussed above had been systematically violated. The leading nations of western Europe put their heads together to identify the rights and freedoms which they regarded as the basic and fundamental entitlement of those living in their respective countries. Prominent in negotiating the treaty were the British and the French. The British, whose institutions and traditions were thought to be vindicated by their victory, did not think they had much to learn, but thought it valuable to share their values with others less fortunate. The French, proud of their 1789 Declaration of the Rights of Man and the Citizen, similarly thought they had little to learn. Both were to find that not all the beams were in the eyes of others.

Over the past decade or so, the Human Rights Act and the Convention to which it gave effect in the UK have been attacked in some quarters, and of course there are court decisions, here and in the European Court, with which one may reasonably disagree. But most of the supposed weaknesses of the Convention scheme are attributable to misunderstanding of it, and critics must ultimately answer two questions. Which of the rights discussed above would you discard? Would you rather live in a country in which these rights were not protected by law? I repeat the contention with which this chapter opens: the rule of law requires that the law afford adequate protection of fundamental human rights. It is a good start for public authorities to observe the letter of the law, but not enough if the law in a particular country does not protect what are there regarded as the basic entitlements of a human being. In all countries which are parties to the European Convention the central rights guaranteed by the Convention are protected, although disappointed claimants can still seek to pursue their claims in the European Court at Strasbourg if unsuccessful at home. There are probably rights which could valuably be added to the Convention, but none which could safely be discarded. The most pressing problem now, however, is not whether the scope of the Convention should be enlarged but whether the Strasbourg court can handle the huge volume of cases currently brought before it.[46]

8

Dispute Resolution

(6) Means must be provided for resolving, without prohibitive cost or inordinate delay, bona fide civil disputes which the parties themselves are unable to resolve

It would seem to be an obvious implication of the principle that everyone is bound by and entitled to the protection of the law that people should be able, in the last resort, to go to court to have their civil rights and claims determined. An unenforceable right or claim is a thing of little value to anyone.

In Utopia, it may be, civil disputes would never arise: the citizens would live together in amity, and harmony would reign. But we live in a sub-utopian world, in which differences do arise, and it would be false to suppose that they only arise when there is dishonesty, sharp practice, malice, greed or obstinacy on one side or the other. Those qualities are not, of course, unknown among litigants. But it is possible for perfectly reasonable and well-motivated people to hold very different views on the meaning of a contract or a conveyance or a will, or about the responsibility for an accident, or about the upbringing of children following their parents' separation, or about the use of a footpath, or the application of an Act of Parliament or the decision of a minister or local government officer. And then the need is for a binding decision. It is not in the interests of those involved in the dispute or of society as a whole that victory should go to the stronger (in modern terms, the party who can send in the best-armed heavies).

Nothing that I say here should be understood as discouraging or disparaging resort to what are sometimes called 'alternative' but are better called 'additional' means of resolving disputes. One of these, in very many ways the best means of resolving civil disputes, is mediation or conciliation. This process involves the engagement of an independent mediator or conciliator, who will explore the parties' competing views and aims and try to coax them into reaching a mutually acceptable compromise. If this is achieved, neither party is completely happy because neither, probably, has gained all that he or she hoped for, but neither suffers the distress and humiliation of losing completely and the unpleasantness of antagonistic litigation. A settlement that is agreed is likely to be more readily honoured than one that is imposed. If no compromise is achieved (and it often is) the parties have wasted some time and some money, but less of both than if they had gone to court.

An alternative to mediation and conciliation is arbitration: the appointment of an independent arbitrator, often chosen by the parties, to rule on their dispute according to the terms of reference they give him. This can only be done by agreement, before or after the dispute arises, but where it is done the arbitrator has authority to make an award which is binding on the parties and enforceable by the process of the courts.

There are, however, cases in which the parties, having tried to resolve their differences between themselves, fail to do so; when they cannot agree on a process of mediation or conciliation, or the process leads to no compromise; when they cannot or do not agree to arbitrate; and in which the clear need is for a public and authoritative ruling of the court: as, for example, when the meaning of an Act of Parliament, or a standard form of commercial contract, or the lawfulness of official conduct, is in question. Then the rule of law requires that there should be access to a court. In meeting this requirement, most legal systems (and certainly the British) face two potent and enduring obstacles. The first is expense, the second delay.

It has been said, with heavy irony, that justice in the UK is open to all, like the Ritz Hotel. This is not a new complaint. Three hundred and fifty years ago it was said: 'Every man complains of the horrible delays in matters of justice . . . The remedy is worse than the disease . . . A man must spend above £10 to recover £5.'[1] The source of the problem is clear: few people are competent to assess the strength of a claim and conduct litigation without professional help; but solicitors and barristers, like plumbers and electricians, ordinarily charge a fee; and since litigation is highly labour-intensive, with even a small case usually demanding more hours of work than, for instance, the longest surgical operation, the cost tends to be high. The Scots recognized this problem as long ago as 1424 when, in the world's first statutory authority on legal aid for the poor, it was enacted that, 'If there be any poor creature for default of cunning or means that cannot or may not follow his course', free legal assistance should be given to him. Seventy years later the English followed suit,[2] but neither scheme was entirely satisfactory.[3] In the late nineteenth century, in a surge of practical philanthropy characteristic of the late Victorians, a number of free legal advice centres (originally known as 'Poor Man's Lawyers'), manned by volunteers, were established at the Mansfield House Settlement and Toynbee Hall in the East End of London, and in other deprived areas of the country.[4] But there was growing recognition of a large unmet need, strengthened by the criticism of refugee scholars with experience of Continental systems, where better provision was made. One of these, Dr E. J. Cohn, made the case with compelling clarity:

Legal aid is a service which the modern state owes to its citizens as a matter of principle. It is part of the protection of the citizen's individuality which, in our modern conception of the relationship between the citizen and the State, can be claimed by those citizens who are too weak to protect themselves. Just as the modern State tries to protect the poorer classes against the common dangers of life, such as unemployment, disease, old age, social oppression, etc., so it should protect them when legal difficulties arise. Indeed, the case for such protection is stronger than the case for any other form of protection. The State is not responsible for the outbreak of epidemics, for old age or economic crises. But the State is responsible for the law. That law again is made for the protection of all citizens, poor and rich alike. It is therefore the duty of the State to make its machinery work alike, for the rich and the poor.[5]

The pressure for reform culminated in the Legal Aid and Advice Act 1949, one of the great but less-celebrated achievements of the post-war Attlee government. For half a century the legal aid scheme enabled those without means to sue and defend themselves in the courts. The scheme was not without faults: it led to the public financing of too many unmeritorious claims, and it bore hardly on privately funded defendants. But its cost was its undoing. In the years 1988 to 1996/7 expenditure on civil (and also criminal) legal aid rose at a rate substantially in excess of inflation, and was the fastest rising item of government expenditure overall. So, perhaps ironically, it fell to the New Labour government to restrain access to civil legal aid, seeking to substitute conditional fee agreements and certain forms of insurance. Despite determined efforts, led by Lord Woolf, to reduce the cost of civil litigation, and the introduction of admirable pro bono (gratuitous) schemes by solicitors and barristers, there must be concern that there now exists, once again, a large unmet need.

If denial of legal protection to the poor litigant who cannot afford to pay is one enemy of the rule of law, delay in affording a remedy is another. It is a familiar aphorism, attributed to Gladstone,[6] that 'justice delayed is justice denied', and King John famously pledged in Magna Carta that he would neither deny nor delay justice. But four centuries later Hamlet even more famously listed 'the law's delay' as one of the reasons for committing suicide,[7] and any litigant in the early nineteenth-century Court of Chancery, as accurately depicted by Dickens in *Bleak House*, could be forgiven for taking the step from which Hamlet drew back. It is no doubt desirable that judges should deliberate on their judgments with care, but to do so for years on end, as was the practice of Lord Eldon in the early nineteenth century,[8] in cases which had no doubt taken years to reach him, was to exceed a tolerable period for reflection by a huge margin.

There is no equivalent of the nineteenth-century Court of Chancery in the UK today. But despite repeated efforts to expedite the process of litigation, most recently led, again, by Lord Woolf, delay remains a bugbear, and the periods of delay complained of in cases reaching Strasbourg from the UK (nearly nine years in one case) should cure any temptation to be complacent.[9] It is not enough to point to even longer delays occurring elsewhere.

Delay is not only undesirable in itself but also exacerbates the problem of expense, since experience clearly shows that the longer a case drags on the more it costs. It some countries, notably Italy, the problem of delay is extreme. It is also a source of complaint about the European Court of Justice at Luxembourg, where the average time to rule on requests by member states for preliminary rulings at the end of 2007 was 19.3 months; for direct actions it was 18.2 months and for appeals 17.8 months. In the Court of First Instance, established to ease pressure on the European Court of Justice, the average time taken for a case to be completed was 29.5 months in ordinary procedures.[10] These lengthy periods of delay are not the result of sloth in the Luxembourg courts and their judges. They are the result of three things: the success of the courts, leading to an increased workload; the enlargement of the Community; and the burden of translation. There are now, after recent expansion, twenty-three working languages in the European Union, and the average delay in each case caused by translation alone is seven months.[11] Delays of this order are generally agreed to be unacceptable, and one knowledgeable commentator has said: 'For a merger appeal to have any value for business, the maximum time taken to deliver a judgment should be six months.'[12]

The goal of expeditious and affordable resolution of civil disputes is elusive, and likely to remain so. This is so particularly in common law countries like the UK (and the United States, Canada, Australia, India, etc.) as compared with civil law countries (like France and Germany). This is because the adversarial procedure adopted in common law courts is heavily dependent on expensive lawyers preparing, presenting and arguing the case. They are expected to lay before the judge all the material necessary to decide the case and the judge, as neutral referee, has to decide which case he prefers. In civil law countries, the role of the lawyers (paid by the parties) is much smaller, and that of the judge (paid by the state) much larger. The civil law judge has greater control over the proceedings than his common law counterpart. Even in civil law countries, the goal of expeditious and affordable dispute resolution is hard to achieve. But the closer a country comes to achieving this goal, the better (in this respect) the rule of law is served.

9

A Fair Trial

(7) Adjudicative procedures provided by the state should be fair

The right to a fair trial is a cardinal requirement of the rule of law. It is a right to be enjoyed, obviously and pre-eminently, in a criminal trial, but the rather ponderous language of this principle is chosen to make clear that the right extends beyond a criminal trial. It applies to civil trials, whoever is involved, whether private individuals or companies or public authorities. It applies to adjudicative procedures of a hybrid kind, not criminal but not civil in the ordinary sense either: proceedings in which one or more parties may suffer serious consequences if an adverse decision is made. There is no requirement that these three forms of proceeding should follow the same pattern, and in practice they do not. But there are some principles which apply to all three.

First, it must be recognized that fairness means fairness to both sides, not just one. The procedure followed must give a fair opportunity for the prosecutor or claimant to prove his case as also to the defendant to rebut it. A trial is not fair if the procedural dice are loaded in favour of one side or the other, if (in the phrase used in the European cases) there is no equality of arms.[1] This is sometimes overlooked, and evidence is not infrequently the subject of objection in criminal trials as 'prejudicial' when the real basis of the objection is simply that it is damaging to the defence. In truth, of course, almost all prosecution evidence is, or is intended to be, damaging to the defence.

It must, secondly, be accepted that fairness is a constantly evolving concept, not frozen at any moment of time. This is most obviously true of criminal trials. It was only in 1836, after failures in 1821, 1824, 1826 and 1834, that a measure was introduced granting defence counsel (if the accused was lucky enough to be represented) the right to address the jury on his behalf.[2] So the prosecutor could tell the jury why the defendant was guilty, but there was no advocate to say why he was not. Mr Justice Hawkins, in his *Reminiscences*,[3] recalled a defendant convicted of theft at the Old Bailey in the 1840s after a trial which lasted two minutes fifty-three seconds, including an economical jury direction: 'Gentlemen, I suppose you have no doubt? I have none.' Not until just over a century ago was the defendant entitled to give evidence at his own trial. For the first thirty years of the twentieth century attempts to provide legal assistance for criminal defendants who could not afford it were largely frustrated by official hostility and the obstructiveness of magistrates and judges.[4] Well after the middle of the century, it was the practice of some trial judges to sum up to juries in favour of conviction in highly tendentious, sometimes even rhetorical, terms, mitigated only by reminders that of course the facts were a matter for the jury. In even more recent times, the lack of an obligation on the prosecution to disclose material in their possession has led to notorious miscarriages of justice. In some countries (some of the Southern States of the United States and parts of the Caribbean), the poor quality of defence representation is a source of unfairness. A time is unlikely to come when anyone will ever be able to say that perfect fairness has been achieved once and for all, and in retrospect most legal systems operating today will be judged to be defective in respects not yet recognized.

The constitution of a modern democracy governed by the rule of law must, thirdly, guarantee the independence of judicial decision-makers, an expression I use to embrace all those making decisions of a judicial character, whether they are judges (or jurors or magistrates) or not. Acceptance of this principle, as a principle, is widespread. In the UK, as briefly recounted in Chapter 2, the keel of judicial independence was laid in the Act of Settlement 1701, which effectively protected the judges against dismissal by the government without good cause. Further protection is codified in the Constitutional Reform Act 2005, which provides in section 3(1) that 'The Lord Chancellor, other Ministers of the Crown and all with responsibility for matters relating to the judiciary or otherwise to the administration of justice must uphold the continued independence of the judiciary.' Section 3(5) goes further: 'The Lord Chancellor and other Ministers of the Crown must not seek to influence particular judicial decisions through any special access to the judiciary.' The Lord Chancellor must also have regard to the need to defend judicial independence, and must swear an oath to defend it. The Lord Chancellor was in the past a judge, the head of the judiciary and the minister responsible for appointing the senior judges in England and Wales. Since 2003 he has not been a judge, and since 2005 he has no longer been head of the judiciary. His role in the appointment of judges is also much reduced. But the Lord Chancellor has also, since 2005, been Secretary of State for Justice, and he carries the major ministerial responsibility for the integrity of the justice system. He still comes into frequent contact with the judges. In the quoted sections of the 2005 Act it is judges in the strict sense who are referred to, but independence is essential to the integrity of all decision-makers in the fields under discussion, not just judges.

These statutory references make clear that judges must be independent of ministers and the government. Does the principle require independence of anyone or anything other than the government? It does. It calls for decision-makers to be independent of local government, vested interests of any kind, public and parliamentary opinion, the media, political parties and pressure groups, and their own colleagues, particularly those senior to them. In short, they must be independent of anybody or anything which might lead them to decide issues coming before them on anything other than the legal and factual merits of the case as, in the exercise of their own judgment, they consider them to be. There would be an obvious threat to that independence if a decision-maker's salary or tenure of office were dependent on the acceptability of his judgments to those affected by them. A similar threat would arise if (as has happened in other countries but scarcely ever, in recent years, in the UK) a decision-maker's prospects of promotion could be blighted because his judgments were unwelcome to the powers that be.

Scarcely less important than an independent judiciary is an independent legal profession, fearless in its representation of those who cannot represent themselves, however unpopular or distasteful their case may be.

Closely allied to the requirement of independence is the requirement that a decision-maker be impartial. The European Convention requires a tribunal to be both independent and impartial. This means that the decision-maker, to the greatest extent possible, should approach the issues with an open mind, ready to respond to the legal and factual merits of the case. A decision-maker who is truly independent of all influences extraneous to the case to be decided is likely to be impartial, but may nonetheless be subject to personal predilections or prejudices which may pervert his judgment. Of course, since judges and other decision-makers are human beings and not robots, they are inevitably, to some extent, the product of their own upbringing, experience and background. The mind which they bring to the decision of issues cannot be a blank canvas. But they should seek to alert themselves to, and so neutralize, any extraneous considerations which might bias their judgment, and if they are conscious of bias, or of matters which might give rise to an appearance of bias, they must decline to make the decision in question. In all this, Sir Matthew Hale (who featured in Chapter 2) was ahead of his time.

Historically, relations between judges and the government in this country were much closer than they are today, and the most senior judicial offices were held by political appointees. Today the UK has a professional judiciary which is as non-political as any in the world, and appointments are made on the recommendation of independent selection boards, which consult widely but have no political representatives. This does not prevent close and friendly co-operation on an administrative level, which is essential to the smooth running of the courts, but it ensures that the judges' decisions are theirs alone.

In this connection three cautionary tales may be pertinent. The first relates to a legislative proposal made in Britain in 1928 which would, if enacted, have permitted a minister, if it appeared to him that a substantial question of law had arisen, to submit the question to the High Court, which, after hearing such parties as it thought proper, would give its opinion on the question.[5] The proposal was the subject of a sustained attack by the judicial members of the House of Lords. The thrust of the criticism was expressed by one judge (Lord Merrivale), who said: 'It is no part of the business of His Majesty's judges, and never has been part of their business, at any rate since the Act of Settlement, to have any advisory concern in the acts of the Administration; or to take any part in advising the Administration.'[6] The vice in the proposal is not hard to see. If judges, almost certainly on hypothetical facts, advise the government that a certain course of conduct would be lawful, they disable themselves from ruling on the question in an independent and impartial way when, in due course, a litigant, on real facts, challenges the lawfulness of the conduct. But at least the 1928 proposal involved an opinion of the High Court, given in public and on the record. Far more objectionable would be any undisclosed discussion between judges and the government concerning the lawfulness of a potential course of action. The judge would be similarly disqualified to sit, but the litigant would lack the materials necessary to challenge the independence and impartiality of the judge, if the judge did not declare his interest and disqualify himself of his own accord. Obvious though it is, recent experience suggests that this is not a point which all ministers understand.

A rule of political neutrality in the judiciary has not been universally observed in the past, and is not now. Notably is this true in the United States, where federal (including Supreme Court) judges and justices are appointed on the nomination of the President, provided the Senate consent. Thus the President can usually secure the appointment of judges who share his own political views. Justice Brandeis was a major architect of President Woodrow Wilson's legislative programme. During the Second World War, Justice Frankfurter conferred almost daily with President Roosevelt about strategies and policies, and assisted in drafting some of the President's speeches. Justice Fortas advised President Lyndon Johnson on topics including the Vietnam War, steel price increases and strategy for averting transport strikes.[7] When he was Chief Justice of Australia (1952–64), the greatly respected Sir Owen Dixon advised state governors on constitutional questions and the Commonwealth government on foreign policy questions in a way which, as an Australian newspaper observed in 2003, 'would now be considered wildly inappropriate'.[8] In the United States, as is well known, the appointment of Supreme Court justices is a matter of acute political controversy, and the Supreme Court's decision in

Bush v Gore, ensuring the success of George W. Bush in the 2000 presidential election, has been described as a display of 'simple political partisanship'.[9] In Britain, the rule of law is held to require the strictest political neutrality of the judges.

The second cautionary tale (to which I was alerted by Professor Vernon Bogdanor, Professor of Government at Oxford) concerns the watershed judgment of the United States Supreme Court in perhaps its most admired civil rights decision: *Brown v Board of Education*,[10] when the court held racial segregation in public (meaning not-private) schools to be unconstitutional. It was 1954 and Eisenhower was the President. According to his biographer, while the case was current,

He [Eisenhower] invited Warren [the Chief Justice] to the White House for a stag dinner, along with Brownell [the Attorney General of the United States], John W. Davis, who was counsel for the segregationists, and a number of other lawyers. Eisenhower had Davis sit near Warren, who in turn was on the President's right hand. During dinner, Eisenhower – according to Warren – 'went to considerable lengths to tell me what a great man Davis was'. And as the guests were filing out of the dining room, Eisenhower took Warren by the arm and said of the southerners, 'These are not bad people. All they are concerned about is to see that their sweet little girls are not required to sit in school alongside some big overgrown Negroes.'[11]

It appears that counsel for Brown, whether invited or not, was absent. Happily, Warren was impervious to the pressure put on him by the President, and gave the judgment in favour of Brown. But even fifty years later one must be shocked that Eisenhower acted as he apparently did. He did not resist implementation of the judgment, and indeed took firm action to enforce it, although in Warren's view it was the end of cordial relations between the two men. It was disapproval of the Warren court's criminal decisions which led Eisenhower to say, much later, that his biggest mistake was 'the appointment of that dumb son of a bitch Earl Warren'.[12] I do not think that any comparable attempt to influence a judicial decision in the UK has been made by the executive for very many years.

My third cautionary tale is more recent. It illustrates the pitfalls of combining a political and a judicial role, even though the individual involved – Lord Hardie, a Scots judge – did not act dishonourably in any way or lay himself open to personal criticism.[13] Before becoming a judge in 2000, Lord Hardie was the Lord Advocate, an old and respected office in the Scottish legal system, analogous in many ways to the Attorney General in England, Wales and Northern Ireland. As Lord Advocate he was responsible for handling the passage of the Scotland Bill (which became the Scotland Act 1998, providing for Scottish devolution) through the House of Lords. An amendment was proposed to provide that an injunction or an order for specific performance could not be made against the Crown. Thus the government could not be ordered by the court to do something. Lord Hardie firmly resisted this amendment, saying that the law of Scotland was completely clear on the point and the amendment was unnecessary. It was withdrawn. A few years later, a party to proceedings in Scotland contended that an injunction or an order of specific performance could be made against the Crown. The judge decided against him. He appealed. One of the judges hearing the appeal in 2002 was Lord Hardie, and the appeal was dismissed. At that stage the parties did not know of the earlier exchange in the House of Lords, and Lord Hardie did not mention it. But when the appellant learned of it he challenged the decision of the appeal court, contending that Lord Hardie's earlier involvement gave an appearance of bias which invalidated the court's decision. This contention was accepted in 2005 by the appeal court, which quashed the decision, and was also accepted by the House of Lords. Had Lord Hardie thought to disclose his earlier involvement there would probably have been no problem.

Criminal trials

The right to a fair criminal trial has been described as 'the birthright of every British citizen'.[14] It has also been said to be 'axiomatic that a person charged with having committed a criminal offence should receive a fair trial and that, if he cannot be tried fairly for that offence, he should not be tried for it at all'.[15] Yet again, the right to a fair trial has been described as 'fundamental and absolute'.[16] Over the centuries a framework of rules has grown up, developing over time, to protect the fairness of the trial. Two of the rules, that the court (whether judge, or judge and jury) must be independent and impartial, have already been noticed. A third rule is that the trial should, largely if not wholly, be held and judgment given in public. A fourth rule, applicable in Britain and (contrary to widespread belief) throughout continental Europe, is that a defendant is presumed to be innocent until he is proved to be guilty. To these fundamentals the European Convention has attached a series of minimum additional rights of a specific kind, none of them in any way unfamiliar in the UK before the Convention, although elaborated since.[17] The defendant must be clearly and intelligibly told exactly what crime he is said to have committed. He must have enough time and the facilities he needs to prepare his defence. He must be permitted to defend himself or to be represented by a lawyer of his choice; if he cannot afford legal representation, it must be provided free when the interests of justice require it. He must have the opportunity to examine or have examined witnesses against him and to obtain the attendance and evidence of witnesses on his behalf in the same way as evidence is given against him. He must have the help of an interpreter if the case is conducted in a language he cannot understand. He is entitled to disclosure of material which is helpful to him because it weakens the prosecution case or strengthens his. All these rights would, I think, strike most people as a very basic entitlement. But there are problematic areas.

What if the defendant is tried, convicted and sentenced in his absence? The ordinary rule in the UK is that a defendant (unless removed for misbehaviour in court) should attend his trial, but the judge has a limited discretion to allow the trial to start or continue in his absence provided the judge is satisfied that the defendant has absented himself from the trial of his own free will, and also that the trial can be fairly conducted in his absence, a condition which will rarely be met unless the absent defendant is represented in his absence by a fully instructed lawyer.[18] In some other countries the practice is different. Marcel Berlins, the highly respected (and respectable) legal commentator of the BBC and the *Guardian*, has recounted how, on arriving in an (unidentified) European country, he was arrested and told that he had been tried, convicted and sentenced to a year's imprisonment a few years before for a crime of which he did not know he had ever been accused, at a trial he had had no idea was taking place.[19] This is not necessarily inconsistent with the rule of law if – a very big if – a person tried, convicted and sentenced in such circumstances has an unfettered right, on being apprehended, to be retried as if there had been no earlier trial, or to pursue an appeal at a full rehearing. Berlins records that 'After a few days in custody I was allowed to appeal and things were more or less sorted out', so his position may not have been worse than if he had been arrested and prosecuted for the first time on arrival. But the possibility of being condemned to even a nominal sentence of imprisonment at a trial one never knew was afoot runs counter to British instincts.

More troublesome, because more often encountered in practice, is the problem which arises when the prosecution hold material which is helpful to the defendant, and therefore ought to be disclosed to him, but which the prosecution are unwilling to disclose to him because they consider that it would be seriously damaging to the public interest to do so. It may, for instance, reveal the name of an informer, who would be at personal risk if his identity were known, or may reveal details of secret police operations, or secrets relating to defence. Or, in a child abuse case, for instance, it may reveal very sensitive information held by a social services department relating to a child and sources of information about him. The difficulty is obvious: the defendant's right to a fair trial may be compromised if the material is not disclosed to him, the public interest jeopardized if it is. The judge must decide, on application to him, whether disclosure should be ordered or not. But that in itself is problematic, because the defence does not know what the material is which the prosecution wish to withhold, so that they may have difficulty making a reasoned objection; they may not, in an extreme case, know that an application is being made to the judge at all. This involves a departure from the central principle that the whole trial is conducted in the presence of the defendant and his representatives and that the judge knows nothing which is not known to all the parties. Any such departure is ground for concern. If the judge is satisfied that the material in question really does help the defendant and also that disclosure really would damage a significant aspect of the public interest, and that partial disclosure or a summary of the material omitting the damaging information cannot solve the problem, he has a difficult judgment to make: whether the trial can proceed fairly if the defendant does not have access to the material. If he decides that it can, he will allow the material to be withheld, continuing to monitor the fairness of the trial as it goes along. If he decides that it cannot, he will order disclosure and the prosecution must then disclose the material or abandon the prosecution. This is an unwelcome procedure, but it is thought to comply with the defendant's right to a fair trial under the European Convention.[20]

A very recent case[21] highlighted an even more worrying departure from the practice that has been followed in this country for centuries. It arose from a fatal shooting of two men at the end of an all-night New Year's Eve party. Appearances were against the defendant, who had gone to the United States on a false passport after the killings and, when brought back to this country, declined to answer any questions. But when he stood trial at the Old Bailey on two counts of murder an unusual procedure was adopted. Seven witnesses claimed to be in fear for their lives if it became known that they had given evidence against the defendant. Among the seven were the only witnesses in the case who identified the defendant as the gunman. Their evidence was essential if the defendant was to be convicted. He admitted he had been at the party, but said he had left before the killings. So the case hinged on the evidence of identification. The trial judge accepted that the fears of the witnesses were genuine, and that was thereafter accepted. To ensure the safety of the witnesses, and induce them to give evidence without being ordered to do so, the judge made a series of orders. The witnesses were each to give evidence under a false name. The addresses and personal details of the witnesses, and any particulars which might identify the witnesses, were to be withheld from the defendant and his legal advisers. The defendant's counsel was to ask the witnesses no question which might enable any of them to be identified. The witnesses were to give evidence behind screens so that they could be seen by the judge and the jury but not by the defendant. The witnesses' natural voices were to be heard by the judge and the jury but were to be heard by the defendant and his counsel subject to mechanical distortion, so as to prevent recognition by the defendant. The defendant's counsel could himself have seen the witnesses, but he was not allowed to describe them to the defendant and properly chose to receive no information which he could not share with him. The effect of this procedure, in a case which depended crucially on the accuracy and honesty of the evidence identifying the defendant, was to deny him any opportunity of effectively challenging it. He simply did not know who was accusing him. Without knowing that, he could scarcely begin to defend himself. The obvious questions ('How long have you known the defendant? How well did you know him? Where did you meet him?') could not be asked.

The old rule established at common law (and reflected in the European Convention) was that a defendant in a criminal trial should be confronted by and entitled to cross-examine prosecution witnesses. As noted in Chapter 2, the Constitution of the United States, by the Sixth Amendment, guarantees this. Parliament had not, at the time of the Old Bailey trial just described, legislated to modify this rule, although it has done so since. But the judge in this case did not strike out on a novel path of his own: he followed a practice which had gradually developed, in a series of judicial rulings, since about 1990. So he was following what was fast becoming a beaten track. But on analysis none of these rulings supported the procedure adopted in this case. The inescapable question underlying the case was, therefore, a short one: did the procedure adopted deny the defendant a fair trial? The trial judge held it did not, and the Court of Appeal agreed with him. But the House of Lords unanimously held that it did, whether judged by the common law or the European Convention. It was a procedure plainly inconsistent with the rule of law, since there was no lawful authority to adopt it and it effectively destroyed the defendant's right to a fair trial. So the defendant's appeal succeeded. He was liable to be retried, but the prosecution was unlikely to succeed unless evidence to identify the defendant as the murderer could be adduced.

Civil actions

Historically, the parties to a civil action in the UK could to a large extent keep their powder dry until the trial, a procedure which came to be known colloquially as 'trial by ambush'. But the rules have changed. The fair trial of a civil action is now held to require the parties to reveal their respective cases and almost all material relevant to them before the trial even begins. The policy of the law is that litigation should be conducted with the 'cards face up on the table'. This is achieved, first, by requiring the claimant to set out in writing in some detail the grounds on which he claims. He cannot appear at trial and present a case different from that which he has advanced in writing. The defendant in turn must set out in some detail in writing the grounds on which he resists the claim. He cannot simply deny the claim and leave the claimant and the judge wondering what his defence is. Nor can he appear at trial and advance a defence different from that indicated. Thus the line of battle should be drawn with some precision before the first shot is fired in court.

The parties are, secondly, required to disclose to each other any documents on which they rely in the action and any documents which adversely affect their own cases, any documents which adversely affect any other party's case or any documents which support any other party's case.[22] This is a very important procedure, since it means that a party may not produce the documents which strengthen his case while withholding the documents which weaken it, and not infrequently letters, diary entries, memos and minutes made or written at the time provide a surer guide to the truth than what the litigants say years later when differences have arisen. Lawyers often hope, usually vainly, that among the other side's documents there will be one or two documents which will demolish that party's case, but documents disclosed in this way can be very revealing, and litigants are often surprised by the intrusiveness of the procedure. Material cannot be withheld even if it is extremely personal.

Nowadays, in contrast with practice in the past, the parties are required, thirdly, to exchange in advance the statements of the witnesses they propose to call. The days of the mystery witness, unexpectedly called at the eleventh hour to reveal all, are a thing of the past, a great loss to television drama but a great gain to justice. A party cannot lie low and ambush his opponent.

The general rule of documentary disclosure is subject to certain limited exceptions, of which two should be mentioned. The first is sometimes described as 'legal professional privilege', an unhappy misnomer since it wrongly suggests that the privilege belongs to the legal profession when in truth it belongs to the client. The purpose of this exemption from the duty of disclosure is to protect the quality and confidentiality of legal advice given to the client. To this end, it has been said,

it is necessary that actual and potential litigants . . . should be free to unburden themselves without reserve to their legal advisers, and their legal advisers be free to give honest and candid advice on a sound factual basis, without fear that these communications may be relied on by an opposing party if the dispute comes before the court for decision. It is the protection of confidential communications between client and legal adviser which lies at the heart of legal professional privilege . . .[23]

It is an exemption which the client, because it belongs to him, may choose to waive, but the lawyer, because it does not belong to him, may not.

A second ground of exemption arises where one party holds material which is relevant to the issues in the action, and ought therefore ordinarily to be disclosed, but that party claims that disclosure would injure the public interest in a significant respect.[24] This ground is closely analogous to that already noted in the context of criminal trials and in both contexts is now labelled 'public interest immunity' or 'PII'. The party which holds the material, if it considers that the potential damage to the public interest in disclosure outweighs the potential damage to the interests of justice which would be caused by non-disclosure, makes application to withhold it. The judge must decide, usually after reading the material (which the other side will not, of course, have seen). He must weigh up where the balance of the public interest lies. The result of granting the application and refusing to order disclosure may be to defeat the action altogether. But the judge may decide that the damage to the interests of justice if the material is withheld outweighs the public interest in keeping the material secret, and then he will order disclosure. It is another uncomfortable situation since again, if the trial goes ahead without disclosure, the judge knows something which one of the parties does not.

A real case, finally decided in 1977, illustrates the problem.[25] The NSPCC, having received a report that a mother was seriously abusing her child, sent an inspector to the house. The inspector interviewed the mother and examined the child, but found nothing amiss and the NSPCC did not pursue the matter. But the parents of the child were, understandably enough, deeply upset and shocked by the complaint. They started an action against the NSPCC claiming damages for negligence. Their real object, however, was to discover the identity of the informant. This the NSPCC refused to reveal, claiming that this information fell within the public interest immunity exception: the work done by the Society to protect children would, it said, be gravely hampered if members of the public (who might be family members, neighbours, teachers or friends) could not give it information in total confidence that their identity would never be revealed. If, as was accepted, this complaint was malicious, that did not alter the principle. In this instance, none of the courts hearing the case read the document revealing the name, and I (as counsel for the NSPCC) did not know it either. The House of Lords, where the case ended, decided in favour of the NSPCC. So the name did not have to be revealed. The result was that the parents' case collapsed.

Hybrid procedures

There are some procedures which are not criminal in the usual sense, because the defendant is not accused of having committed a crime and is not liable to be punished if an adverse order is made (although it may feel like punishment to him), but yet the proceeding is not one in which the usual civil remedies (damages, or an injunction, or a declaration) are sought. Rather, the issue may be whether a person represents a danger to the public such that he should be kept under, or made subject to, a measure of restraint. Usually such an issue arises in a context which may well raise very difficult factual issues but no legally problematical questions, as where a compulsorily detained mental patient seeks to be discharged from a mental hospital on the ground that he has recovered, or a prisoner eligible for release on parole but not entitled to demand it seeks to show that there is no real risk of his committing an offence if released. To such hearings the principles outlined above, adapted as appropriate in the particular circumstances, apply to ensure that hearings are fair.

Even parole board hearings, held to decide whether a prisoner may safely be released, may raise problems of the kind just discussed if the authorities seek to resist the grant of parole on grounds which are disclosed to the members of the parole board but not to the prisoner and those representing him. This may be illustrated by the recent case of Harry Roberts.[26]

Harry Roberts was convicted on three counts of murder in December 1966, having pleaded guilty to two counts and been convicted of the third. The victims were police officers, killed in cold blood at Shepherd's Bush in London in August of that year. It was a crime which aroused wide public outrage, and many thought that Roberts should never be released. But the trial judge recommended that he serve a term of at least thirty years, a very long sentence in those days, and the Home Secretary in due course fixed thirty years as the term Roberts was to serve. That term expired in 1996, when he was aged sixty. In 2000, following a recommendation by the Parole Board, Roberts was transferred to an open prison, the usual prelude to (and a preparation for) release. A review of parole began, and in 2001 a dossier of reports, all favourable and recommending his release on life licence, was disclosed to him. Then, suddenly, he was removed from his open prison and returned to a secure prison. He was given a general indication of the allegations against him which led to his removal, but these were not the subject of a criminal charge, or a charge under the disciplinary code which applies to prisoners, were not investigated at any contested adversarial hearing and were denied by Roberts throughout. As preparations for the Parole Board progressed, the Home Secretary (opposing Roberts's release) disclosed some further material to the board and to Roberts. This related to certain breaches of trust which Roberts was said to have committed while in open conditions. But Roberts was also told that further material was to be put before the board for its consideration which would not be disclosed to him. The reason for adopting this course did not relate to national security: it was that the safety of the source of the material would be at risk if the material were to be disclosed. The board decided to receive this material, but to appoint a special advocate to represent Roberts. The special advocate was to be in an unusual position for a lawyer: he was able to take instructions from Roberts, although Roberts did not know what the secret material contained; he was then to be shown the secret material, on the strict condition that he was to tell Roberts nothing about it; and then, uninstructed by Roberts, he was to represent Roberts, although Roberts and his lawyers were not to be present when the secret material was dealt with. Roberts challenged this procedure. He said the Parole Board had no power to adopt it, and that if it were followed the hearing would be unfair.

The case reached the House of Lords where opinion on the first point was divided, a majority holding that the board did have power to adopt the procedure. A minority disagreed. But for present purposes the second point is more relevant: whether, if the hearing went ahead as planned, it would be a fair hearing. This was considered at some length, and reference was made to earlier rulings. Lord Devlin had described it as 'the fundamental principle of justice that the judge should not look at material that the parties before him have not seen'.[27] Lord Mustill had spoken of 'a first principle of fairness that each party to a judicial process should have an opportunity to answer by evidence and argument any adverse material which the tribunal may take into account when forming its opinion'.[28] The same approach had been taken in cases concerning the Parole Board, and in a string of European cases decided at Strasbourg.[29] Against that background, I expressed doubt whether a decision of the Parole Board adverse to Roberts, based on evidence not disclosed even in outline to him or his legal representatives, which neither he nor they had heard and which neither he nor they had had any opportunity to challenge or rebut, could be held to meet the fundamental duty of procedural fairness required by the Convention.[30] For Lord Woolf the question was 'whether in the particular case there has been a breach of the irreducible minimum standard of fairness'.[31] He said that 'If a case arises where it is impossible for the board both to make use of information that has not been disclosed to the prisoner and, at the same time, protect the prisoner from a denial of his fundamental right to a fair hearing then the rights of the prisoner have to take precedence . . .'.[32] Lord Steyn was characteristically forthright: 'Taken as a whole, the [proposed] procedure completely lacks the essential characteristics of a fair hearing. It is important not to pussyfoot about such a fundamental matter: the special advocate procedure undermines the very essence of elementary justice. It involves a phantom hearing only.'[33] He considered that the procedure would be contrary to the rule of law.[34] Lord Carswell, a former Lord Chief Justice of Northern Ireland with much experience of situations where the lives of informers were at risk, thought it premature to rule on the fairness of the procedure, a view with which most of the other judges agreed,[35] but he accepted that there might well be cases in which the proposed procedure would not be sufficiently fair to be justifiable.[36]

Following this decision, a Parole Board hearing took place at which the secret material was withheld from Roberts and a special advocate protected his interests as best he could. The board made very serious findings against Roberts, and did not recommend release. But then, in an unusual development appropriate for television drama, Roberts received all the secret material through the post from an unknown source. After a further court hearing, the Parole Board held another hearing, this time with no evidence withheld and, thus, no need for a special advocate. For the first time his own counsel was able, effectively, to cross-examine the witnesses against him. The board again reached conclusions which were in many ways highly adverse to Roberts, but they rejected the most damaging allegations which had been found to be proved at the first hearing. This experience, it may be thought, highlights the danger of relying on a special advocate to achieve justice when the crucial information is withheld from the accused individual.

It was not long until the problem arose again, although the context this time was different. Under an Act of Parliament passed in 2005,[37] the Home Secretary had power to make a control order against a person if he had reasonable grounds for suspecting the person to be or have been involved in terrorism-related activity and he considered that it was necessary, to protect the public against the risk of terrorism, to make such an order. The order could not lawfully deprive the controlee of his liberty, but could contain obligations not far short of house arrest: thus the controlee could be required to wear an electronic tag; to live at a specified address; to remain at that address for long hours each day; to be denied all means of outside communication; to go nowhere outside a prescribed area; to meet and be visited by no one the Home Office had not approved; and so on. The cumulative effect of the obligations could render any normal life impossible.

Following the making of such an order there had to be a hearing before a judge at which he would consider whether the Home Secretary's decision to make the order was flawed. It would of course be flawed if there was no evidence reasonably capable of supporting it. But under the Act and rules made under it, no information was to be made available to the controlee or his lawyers if disclosure would be contrary to the public interest. So, as in the case of Mr Roberts (but this time under the express authority of statute), material could be placed before the judge but withheld from the controlee and his lawyers, who would be required to absent themselves when this secret material was considered. A special advocate could be appointed to represent the interests of the controlee, but on the highly restrictive conditions already noted. Again, questions arose whether this procedure gave the controlee a fair hearing.

In one case, known by the initials of the controlee as *MB*,[38] the Home Secretary acknowledged that the case disclosed to him was 'relatively thin' but relied on the confidence of the Security Service that MB had terrorist intentions. The judge observed: 'The basis for the Security Service's confidence is wholly contained within the closed [i.e. secret] material. Without access to that material it is difficult to see how, in reality, [MB] could make any effective challenge to what is, on the open [i.e. disclosed] case before him, no more than a bare assertion.' He concluded that MB had not had a fair hearing. The Court of Appeal disagreed, holding that the appointment of a special advocate was an adequate safeguard of fairness.

In a second case – *AF*[39] – the judge found it clear that the essence of the Home Secretary's case against AF was in the secret material and that AF did not know what the case against him was. The judge accepted without qualification an argument advanced by AF's counsel that no clear or significant allegations of involvement in terrorist-related activity had been disclosed to AF, that no such allegations had been summarized, that the case made by the Home Secretary against AF was in its essence entirely undisclosed to him, and that no allegations of wrongdoing had been put to him by the police in interview after his arrest, affording him by that side wind an idea of what the case against him might be.

The two cases, *MB* and *AF*, came before the House of Lords together. It was clear that the courts in each case had acted in accordance with the Act of Parliament and the rules in receiving and acting on the secret material, but the question was whether the statutory procedure could be consistent with the controlees' fair trial rights under the European Convention. I myself had difficulty in accepting that either MB or AF had had a fair hearing, and most of the judges accepted that the statutory scheme could operate unfairly, even if it would not do so in all cases. The effective decision accordingly was that the scheme should be treated as operable only where it was consistent with fairness for it to be followed. The courts were asked to reconsider the cases on that basis.

It has been accepted that the engagement of special advocates in cases of this kind can improve the level of protection given to people in the position of MB, AF, Roberts and others. A special advocate may be able to show that evidence relied on by the authorities is tainted, unreliable or unsatisfactory. This has been recognized.[40] It is a constructive response to the undoubtedly difficult situation where the case against a person rests on information which it would be dangerous to disclose. But we should not lose sight of three points. The first is the strange relationship between a special advocate and the person whose interests he is appointed to protect. Ordinarily, a lawyer can have no secrets from his client, whom he must advise honestly and candidly on the basis of all that he knows. A special advocate cannot act in that way, and so it is provided that he owes no duty to the person whose interests he is intended to protect. This is, as observed in the House of Lords, a novel relationship, unknown to the law.[41] It is also, as some have found, a very uncomfortable role.

The second point, made by Lord Chief Justice Woolf, is that 'The use of [a special advocate] is, however, never a panacea for the grave disadvantages of a person not being aware of the case against him.'[42] This is by no means an over-statement. Such a procedure may, in some cases, undermine the principle on which adversarial trials and hearings are and should be conducted.

The third point, already made but almost incapable of overemphasis, is this: the right to a fair trial is 'fundamental and absolute'; where a conflict arises between the use of material not disclosed to a party and the right of that party to a fair hearing his right to a fair hearing must prevail. Not every non-disclosure renders a hearing unfair. Questions of degree arise. An adverse decision may be justified on the basis of what is disclosed. What the party does not know may be relatively insignificant compared with what he does. But if the effect of non-disclosure is to render a hearing unfair, the rule of law is violated. After several further hearings, AF's case (with two others) returned to the House of Lords in February–March 2009. An enlarged panel of nine Law Lords was established to hear the appeal, and they gave judgment in June. They held, unanimously, that procedural fairness required a person in AF's position to be given sufficient information about the case against him to enable him to give effective instructions to his lawyer and present any defence he might have.[43] Thus the rule of law was upheld.[44]

10

The Rule of Law in the
International Legal Order

(8) The rule of law requires compliance
by the state with its obligations in
international law as in national law

I used to be much attracted by the description of public international law as 'The Law of Nations'. It seemed to reflect the lustre of Gentili and Grotius, to invest the subject with a grandeur and dignity separating it from the mundane concerns of everyday life, to conjure up a vision of proud and equal sovereigns, declining to bow the knee to one another but condescending to parley through the medium of their immune envoys. I now think, for very much the same reasons and others, that the expression, if not actually pernicious, is better avoided. For although international law comprises a distinct and recognizable body of law with its own rules and institutions, it is a body of law complementary to the national laws of individual states, and in no way antagonistic to them; it is not a thing apart; it rests on similar principles and pursues similar ends; and observance of the rule of law is quite as important on the international plane as on the national, perhaps even more so. Consistently with this, the current Ministerial Code, binding on British ministers, requires them as an overarching duty to 'comply with the law including international law and treaty obligations'.[1]

In his report of 23 August 2004 to the Security Council, the Secretary-General of the United Nations spoke of the rule of law as a concept at the very heart of the organization's mission. He continued:

It refers to a principle of governance in which all persons, institutions and entities, public and private, including the State itself, are accountable to laws that are publicly promulgated, equally enforced and independently adjudicated, and which are consistent with international human rights norms and standards. It requires, as well, measures to ensure adherence to the principles of supremacy of law, equality before the law, accountability to the law, fairness in the application of the law, separation of powers, participation in decision-making, legal certainty, avoidance of arbitrariness and procedural and legal transparency.[2]

Nothing in this formulation points towards a concept different from that familiar in the domestic sphere. Nor does the formulation of Professor William Bishop, who, having posed the question 'What do we mean by "international Rule of Law"?' proceeded to answer the question:

Without precise definition, I believe we could agree that the concept includes reliance on law as opposed to arbitrary power in international relations; the substitution of settlement by law for settlement by force; and the realization that law can and should be used as an instrumentality for the cooperative international furtherance of social aims, in such fashion as to preserve and promote the values of freedom and human dignity for individuals.[3]

He quoted a former president of the American Bar Association:

The rule of law within nations ... connotes the existence of the hundreds of legal rules, the legal procedures, courts, and other institutions which in sum total add up to order and stability, equality, liberty, and individual freedom ... The rule of law among nations means the regulation of mutual intercourse of nations, and international contacts and relations of individuals, by legal concepts, standards, institutions and procedures.[4]

This would suggest that the rule of law in the international order is, to a considerable extent at least, the domestic rule of law writ large. Such an impression is fortified by two further sources. According to Professor Chesterman, '"the international rule of law" may be understood as the application of rule of law principles to relations between States and other subjects of international law'.[5] In their Millennium Declaration the member states of the United Nations resolved to 'strengthen respect for the rule of law in international as in national affairs and, in particular, to ensure compliance by Member States with the decisions of the International Court of Justice, in compliance with the Charter of the United Nations, in cases to which they are parties'.[6]

The analogy, even if inexact, with the domestic situation makes plain, I suggest, why we should favour strict compliance with the law. However much any of us as individuals might relish the opportunity to live our lives free of all legal constraints – whether to pay taxes, observe the Highway Code, obtain planning permission, discharge our debts or refrain from assaulting our next-door neighbour – we know quite well that acceptance of these constraints is the necessary price to be paid for their observance by others and that a society in which no one was subject to such constraints would not be a very congenial one. Then there might indeed be no such thing as society. The same is true in the international sphere. However attractive it might be for a single state to be free of the legal constraints that bind all other states, those states are unlikely to tolerate such a situation for very long and in the meantime the solo state would lose the benefits and protections that international agreement can confer. The rule of the jungle is no more tolerable in a big jungle.

The point is not infrequently made that there is no international legislature, which is, of course, strictly speaking true, and that international law, as a result, lacks the legitimacy which endorsement by a democratic legislature would give. This does not impress me as a very powerful argument. The means by which an obligation becomes binding on a state in international law seem to be quite as worthy of respect as a measure approved, perhaps in haste and without adequate inquiry, perhaps on a narrowly divided vote, by a national legislature. This is true of treaties to which, by signature and ratification, the state has formally and solemnly committed itself. It is true of 'international custom, as evidence of a general practice accepted as law', since the threshold condition – very widespread observance, as a matter of legal obligation – is not easily satisfied. It is true of 'general principles of law recognized by civilized nations',[7] since such principles carry strong prescriptive authority. The failure of a national legislature to annul a treaty, or reject a rule of customary international law, or disown a general principle of law recognized by civilized nations, may properly be relied on as evidence at least of acquiescence.

In his illuminating recent book, *International Law*, Professor Vaughan Lowe QC poses the question: 'Why do people comply with international law?'[8] I pause to draw attention to the premise of his question, which is that by and large people, including of course states, do comply with international law. This is a very important premise, since it is easy, not least for lawyers, to become mesmerized by breaches of the law and overlook the overwhelming mass of transactions which proceed smoothly, routinely and lawfully. In the domestic sphere, goods are bought and sold, land is conveyed, testamentary bequests take effect and people walk unmolested in the streets because the law is clear and departure from it is the exception, not the rule. So it is in the international sphere also, and international law is not, as sometimes supposed, a code more honoured in the breach than in the observance. Indeed, Professor Lowe observes that this 'view, particularly widespread among those whose vision is unsullied by any knowledge or experience of the matter, is hopelessly wrong'.[9] In answering his own question, the Professor relies on the fact that international law is not imposed on states by an external legislature,[10] and suggests that a powerful reason why states do comply, and always have complied, with international law is that they make the rules to suit themselves.[11] They are the rules of a members', not a proprietor's, club. He suggests other reasons also, among them the tendency to err on the side of caution, habit, and the similarity of outlook among many of those who govern the nations and among the high priesthood of international lawyers who advise the chancelleries of the world.[12]

Most potent of all reasons for compliance by states with international law is the sheer necessity of their doing so. The point was well made by Douglas Hurd, in a passage in a 1997 book quoted by Professor Lowe at the outset of his own book:

[N]ation states are ... incompetent. Not one of them, not even the United States as the single remaining super-power, can adequately provide for the needs that its citizens now articulate. The extent of that incompetence has become sharply clearer during this century. The inadequacy of national governments to provide security, prosperity or a decent environment has brought into being a huge array of international rules, conferences and institutions; the only answer to the puzzle of the immortal but incompetent nation state is effective co-operation between those states for all the purposes that lie beyond the reach of any one of them.[13]

The earliest rules of international law can, I think, be attributed to the self-interest of states, the need to do as one would be done by (I have in mind rules such as those governing the duty to comply with treaty obligations, the equality and immunity of sovereigns, or the immunity of diplomatic representatives) and recognition that there are some mischiefs which can only be effectively addressed if addressed by more states than one (such as piracy). But the passage of time has highlighted the number of situations in which a problem cannot be effectively regulated on a national basis. The international regulation of telecommunications, dating back to 1865, and mail services, dating back to 1874, are two examples. The international carriage of goods by sea provides another: shipowners, charterers, shippers and consignees must, to the greatest extent possible, enjoy the same rights and be subject to the same obligations at the port of loading, the port of discharge and any intermediate port of call, not rights and obligations peculiar to the national law of the port in question. Hence the Hague Rules of 1924, as amended by the Brussels Protocol of 1968. Hence too the Warsaw Convention 1929 on carriage by air, amended at The Hague in 1955 and further amended at Montreal in 1999. Hence also the CMR Convention on the Contract for International Carriage of Goods by Road made at Geneva in 1956 and now, no doubt, applying to the juggernauts from eastern Europe which familiarly thunder up and down the motorways of western Europe.

These are far from unimportant examples. They give effect to Lord Mansfield's insight (quoted in Chapter 3) that if commerce is to prosper investors and businessmen must know where they stand, not only in the UK but abroad. Important as they are, however, such examples scarcely scratch the surface of the current need for international co-operation in tackling problems which are national, in the sense that they afflict single states, but also international, in the sense that they afflict more states than one and can only be tackled jointly. I can make no more than cursory reference to some of these.

It is a matter of history that at the Bretton Woods conference, held in 1944 as the Second World War was approaching its end, the Great

Powers sought to lay the foundations of international economic stability in the aftermath of war, a movement which led to establishment of the International Monetary Fund and the World Bank and, less directly, to the General Agreement on Tariffs and Trade. Here were serious, effective and strictly controlled international schemes to promote development, relieve poverty and raise living standards, reinforced by establishment of the International Centre for the Settlement of Investment Disputes and the Multilateral Investment Guarantee Agency. Regional international groups such as the European Union and the Caribbean Commercial Community have many of the same objects. It is hard to suppose that the traumatic market experience which followed the collapse of the American sub-prime mortgage market in 2007–2009 will not strengthen the hands of those who wish to stiffen such international controls as now exist of the conduct and lending practices of international institutions.

The propensity of criminals who have committed a crime in one jurisdiction to fly to another where they hope to escape apprehension is in no way novel. Nor is the making of bilateral treaties for the extradition of such criminals (usually, with some unfortunate exceptions, on a reciprocal basis). But the need to apprehend and try serious criminals has been greatly strengthened by a number of causes: among them are the increased ease, with modern methods of business and means of communication, of committing a crime in one state of which the effects are felt in another; the utter abhorrence now felt for those who commit the most serious of crimes such as genocide, torture and war crimes; and the international activity of that special brand of criminals whom we stigmatize as terrorists, whose acts of violence are not constrained by national boundaries. These cross-border problems call for cross-border solutions, which can only be provided by a coherent body of enforceable international rules. So it is not surprising, for example, to find the member states of the European Union devising a streamlined means (the European arrest warrant) of procuring the surrender of criminals by and to each other, with much less formality and much less scope for delay than was formerly the norm, a system described as providing for the free movement of judgments.[14] It is not surprising that agreement is reached to extend the jurisdiction of national courts to try the most serious offences, such as genocide, torture and war crimes, wherever the crimes were committed. It is not surprising to find the United Nations establishing an International Criminal Court to try the most serious crimes which will not be tried elsewhere, and ad hoc tribunals to try serious crimes committed in the former Yugoslavia and in Rwanda. It is not surprising to find the United Nations urgently calling on member states to take measures to combat the scourge of terrorism.

If international co-operation is the key to successful action against cross-border criminal activity, it is also essential to secure effective protection of the environment. That is so whether one considers the conservation of a scarce natural resource such as fish, or the activity of one state which causes pollution in another or, pre-eminently, the emission of carbon into the atmosphere. In areas such as these the interests of different states are, in one sense, inherently antithetical. All states want to maintain prosperous fishing fleets, free to catch what they can. All wish to encourage profitable activity without restrictive environmental controls. All wish to maintain, and preferably enhance, their prosperity and the living standards of their people. But of course they know that if fish stocks are depleted beyond a certain point, all lose; freedom to pollute may mean liability to be polluted; and each state knows (or ought to know) that other states will not take the stringent steps necessary to control climate change if it does not. None, I think, can doubt that if effective measures are not taken, on an international basis, to combat climate change, new meaning will be given to Keynes's aphorism that in the long run we are all dead.

Even a cursory and incomplete sketch such as this cannot ignore the international protection of human rights. Such international protection is significant, I suggest, for at least five reasons. First, it is founded on values which, if not universally shared, command very wide acceptance throughout most of the world. No other field of law, perhaps, rests so directly on a moral foundation, the belief that every human being, simply by virtue of his or her existence, is entitled to certain very basic, and in some instances unqualified, rights and freedoms.

Secondly, such international protection is relatively new, essentially a post-Second World War phenomenon inspired by the Universal Declaration on Human Rights of 1948 and followed by the International Covenants on Civil and Political Rights and Economic, Social and

Cultural Rights of 1966, a string of later Conventions such as those on the Elimination of All Forms of Racial Discrimination (1966), the Elimination of All Forms of Discrimination against Women (1979) and that on the Rights of the Child (1989), quite apart from regional instruments such as the European and American Conventions and the African and Arab Charters. Such protection as existed before 1945 was largely extended on a national basis.

Thirdly, the closeness of the relationship between the international protection of human rights and the rule of law has been increasingly recognized. Not until 1996 did the Security Council make express reference to the rule of law in the operative paragraph of a resolution;[15] but it has done so very frequently since. By contrast, the European Court of Human Rights first referred to the rule of law in 1975,[16] and has done so with great consistency since. In 2007 twenty-eight judgments of the Court referred to the rule of law, in January and February 2008 alone no fewer than ten.[17] In a judgment of 22 November 2007, the Court declared that 'the rule of law, one of the fundamental principles of a democratic society, is inherent in all the Articles of the Convention'.[18] After a slow start, the European Court of Justice referred in an obiter dictum in 1969 to 'the fundamental human rights enshrined in the general principles of Community law and protected by the Court'.[19] Very soon the European Convention acquired a special and central role as a source for identifying fundamental rights,[20] and a judge of the European Court of Justice (Antonio Tizzano) has written of 'the defining characteristics of a Community that is first of all a community of principles and values at the heart of which are fundamental rights, constitutionalism, democracy and the rule of law'.[21]

Fourthly, the international protection of human rights is important to the rule of law internationally because of the extent to which national courts are drawn into the process of determining questions of international law. And, lastly, it is important because this is a field in which individual claimants feature very prominently, giving the lie to the old belief that the purview of international law is confined to the regulation of inter-state relations.

The notion that there is a great gulf fixed between national and international law is contradicted both by the osmotic absorption of customary international law into national law, as strikingly illustrated by the

Court of Appeal's decision in *Trendtex Trading Corporation v Central Bank of Nigeria*,[22] upheld by the House of Lords in *I Congreso del Partido*[23] (General Pinochet's first appearance on the English forensic scene), but also and even more prominently by the involvement of the national courts, here and elsewhere, in deciding questions of international law. In his very interesting Michael Kirby Lecture in International Law delivered in Canberra in June 2008,[24] Professor James Crawford SC reviewed and compared the activity of the House of Lords and the High Court of Australia in this field over the period 1996–2008, almost the whole span of Justice Kirby's membership of the High Court. His survey showed that over that period the House of Lords had given judgment on questions of international law in forty-nine cases. The breakdown, on his analysis, of the aspects involved was as follows:

- Relation between treaty law and national law — 7
- Relation between customary international law and national law — 1
- Treaty interpretation — 5
- State immunity — 4
- Refugee Convention obligations — 8
- Other international human rights — 12
- Extradition — 6
- Extra-territorial jurisdiction — 3
- Miscellaneous — 3

His last (miscellaneous) heading embraced compensation of the armed forces for injuries sustained abroad, challenge to an arbitral award and inconsistency between decisions of the European Court of Human Rights and domestic case law. The total would have been significantly higher had decisions pertaining to European Community law been included.

For purposes of his comparison, Professor Crawford reviewed the response of the two courts to four problems which both courts addressed. The upshot of the comparison is not important for present purposes, but the problems addressed are, I think, of interest as showing the range of international law problems arising for decision in national courts. One turned on the meaning of 'a particular social group' as a ground of persecution under Article 1A(2) of the 1951 Refugee Convention. On this point the House made what in my opinion (I was not a party to it) was a bold but correct decision in *R v Immigration Appeal Tribunal, ex p. Shah*,[25] followed more recently in *Fornah v Secretary of State for the Home Department*.[26] The first of these cases related to the treatment of married women suspected of adultery in Pakistan, the second to female genital mutilation in Sierra Leone. Those affected were held to be members of a 'particular social group'. A second question discussed by Professor Crawford, also arising under the Refugee Convention, was the applicability of the Convention where the persecution complained of is not by agents of the state. On that issue of interpretation of the Convention the House again ruled.[27] A third issue addressed by Professor Crawford was indefinite executive detention, on which the British courts made decisions relating both to derogation from the European Convention under Article 15 and compatibility with Article 5 ('the *Belmarsh* case')[28] and the justification under Security Council Resolution 1546 and article 103 of the United Nations Charter for detaining an Iraqi/UK national in Iraq (*Al-Jedda*).[29] The fourth of the Professor's examples examined the question, canvassed in both the High Court and the House of Lords, of whether unincorporated treaties could give rise to legitimate expectations of a kind which could constrain official action, an issue on which an initial divergence of view between the two jurisdictions appears to have narrowed.[30] The cases chosen by Professor Crawford for purposes of comparison were, of course, a very small sample. The breadth of the field is made clear in Shaheed Fatima's interesting recent book, *Using International Law in Domestic Courts*,[31] in which the author lists the main practice areas where issues of international law may arise in national courts: they are aviation law, commercial and intellectual property law, criminal law, employment and industrial relations law, environmental law, European treaties, family and child law, human rights law, immigration and asylum law, immunities and privileges, international organizations, jurisdiction, law of the sea, treaties and, finally, warfare and weapons law. In recent years the British courts have ruled on questions arising in most of these areas. The interrelationship of national law and international law, substantively and procedurally, is such that the rule of law cannot plausibly be regarded as applicable on one plane but not on the other.

War

The last of Shaheed Fatima's headings points to what many, encouraged by Grotius, would reasonably regard as the most fundamental preoccupation of international law: the resort to war, the conduct of war and the rights and duties of an occupying power after a war is over (or, in the legal vernacular, the ius ad bellum, the ius in bello and the ius post bellum). In these areas above all, scrupulous observance of the rule of law may be seen to serve the common interest of mankind.

As Professor Sir Michael Howard has observed, 'war, armed conflict between organized political groups, has been the universal norm in human history'.[32] He quotes Sir Henry Maine, who in 1888 wrote that 'War appears to be as old as mankind, but peace is a modern invention.' Sir Henry spoke too soon. The Hague Conferences of 1899 and 1907, while seeking to humanize the conduct of war, recognized the use of force as an available option. The Covenant of the League of Nations discouraged resort to force, but did not prohibit it. Not until the Kellogg–Briand Pact of 1928 (ratified by Germany, the United States, Belgium, France, Britain and its overseas Dominions, Italy, Japan, Poland, Czechoslovakia and Ireland) was there any renunciation of warfare as an option open to states as an instrument of national policy. But the making of the pact did not, over the coming decades, deter Japan from invading Manchuria, Italy from invading Abyssinia, Russia from invading Finland, Germany from invading most of Europe or Japan from invading large swaths of south-east Asia. Clearly it was necessary for the states of the world to make a further attempt to outlaw a practice whose evil results had been so amply demonstrated.

The Charter of the United Nations, adopted in 1945, to which 192 independent states have acceded, did just that. Having enjoined member states to settle their international disputes by peaceful means, it required them in Article 2(4) to 'refrain in their international relations from the threat or use of force against the territorial integrity or political independence of any state, or in any other manner inconsistent with the Purposes of the United Nations'. Primary responsibility for taking prompt and effective action for the maintenance of international peace and security was conferred on the Security Council, which was authorized to act on behalf of member states.[33] Chapter VII of the Charter, covering threats to and breaches of the peace, provides in Article 39 that 'The Security Council shall determine the existence of any threat to the peace, breach of the peace or act of aggression and shall make recommendations, or decide what measures shall be taken in accordance with Articles 41 and 42, to maintain or restore international peace and security.' Article 41 is directed to measures decided on by the Security Council which do not involve the use of armed force. Article 42 is directed to military measures and provides: 'Should the Security Council consider that measures provided for in Article 41 would be inadequate or have proved to be inadequate, it may take such action by air, sea, or land forces as may be necessary to maintain or restore international peace and security . . .'. By Article 51 the right of a state to defend itself was recognized: 'Nothing in the present Charter shall impair the inherent right of individual or collective self-defence if an armed attack occurs against a Member of the United Nations, until the Security Council has taken measures necessary to maintain international peace and security . . .'. This provision has been interpreted in a way very similar to the right of personal self-defence in domestic law: there must be an armed attack on the state or a threat of imminent attack; the use of force must be necessary and other means of meeting or averting the attack unavailable; the response must be proportionate and strictly limited to defence against the attack or threatened attack. There is controversy whether force may exceptionally be used to avert an overwhelming humanitarian catastrophe, but otherwise the law under the Charter is clear: save in self-defence, force may be used if authorized by the Security Council but not otherwise. Unilateral resort to war is replaced by collective decision-making in the Security Council on behalf of all member states.

Despite this apparently clear and unambiguous regime, an American academic author writing in 2005 recorded that in the past twenty-five years the United States had been involved in some forty military actions, including wars in Iraq, Afghanistan and Yugoslavia; regime-changing invasions in Grenada, Panama and Haiti; military assistance to rebel groups in Angola, El Salvador and Nicaragua; and missile attacks in Lebanon, Libya, Yemen and Sudan.[34] Of these, by far the most contentious was the US-led invasion of Iraq in 2003.

It is not at all clear to me what, if any, legal justification of its action the US Government relied on. Prominent figures in the administration made clear their ambition to remove Saddam Hussein and replace his governmental regime,[35] and British officials gave assurances of the UK's support for regime change.[36] But the British Attorney General, Lord Goldsmith QC, was consistent in his advice that while regime change might be a result of disarming Saddam Hussein, it could not in itself be a lawful objective of military action.[37]

Sir Michael Wood, formerly the senior Legal Adviser to the Foreign and Commonwealth Office but now speaking in a purely personal capacity, has said that the British intervention in Iraq raised no great issue of principle: 'The legality of the use of force in March 2003 turned solely on whether or not it had been authorized by the Council. No one disputes that the Council can authorize the use of force. The question was simply whether it had done so. That turned on the interpretation of a series of Security Council resolutions.'[38] This was the approach taken by the Attorney General in his full written advice of 7 March 2003 to the Prime Minister (not made public at the time) and in his more summary statement published on 17 March 2003, a few days before fighting began.

In the earlier opinion the Attorney General addressed in some detail the interrelationship between three Security Council resolutions, respectively numbered 678, 687 and 1441. Resolution 678 was passed in 1991: it built on earlier resolutions calling for the withdrawal of Iraq from Kuwait following its invasion of that country and authorized the use of force to eject Iraq from Kuwait and restore peace and security in the area. This was the authorization of Operation Desert Storm, which drove the Iraqis out of Kuwait. Resolution 687 (1991) brought military operations to an end, imposing conditions on Iraq with regard to weapons of mass destruction and inspection. It suspended but did not revoke resolution 678. Resolution 1441 was adopted unanimously in November 2002. It recorded that Iraq had been and remained in material breach of its obligations under relevant resolutions, including 687. It offered Iraq a final opportunity to comply with its disarmament obligations. It established a stricter inspection regime and provided that further breaches would be reported to the

Security Council for it 'to consider the situation and the need for full compliance with all of the relevant Council resolutions in order to secure international peace and security'. In his earlier opinion the Attorney General considered that resolution 1441 could in principle revive the authority to use force, but only if the Security Council determined that there was a violation of the conditions of the ceasefire sufficiently serious to destroy the basis of it. The Attorney General reviewed the competing arguments: on the one hand, that there was authority to use force if the Council discussed the matter, even if it did not reach a conclusion; on the other, that nothing short of a further Council decision would provide a legitimate basis for using force. He saw force in both arguments, but concluded that resolution 1441 left the position unclear and that the safest legal course would be to secure the adoption of a further resolution to authorize the use of force. A reasonable case could be made that resolution 1441 was capable in principle of reviving the authorization in resolution 678, but the argument could only be sustainable if there were 'strong factual grounds' for concluding that Iraq had failed to take the final opportunity. There would need to be 'hard evidence'.

In his summary statement of 17 March the Attorney General stated that a material breach of resolution 687 revived the authority to use force under resolution 678; that in resolution 1441 the Security Council had determined that Iraq had been and was in material breach of resolution 687; that resolution 1441 had given Iraq a final opportunity to comply with its disarmament obligations and had warned it of serious consequences if it did not comply; that the Council had also decided in resolution 1441 that any failure to co-operate in implementing resolution 1441 would be a further material breach; that it was 'plain' that Iraq had failed to comply and therefore was at the time of resolution 1441 and continued to be in material breach; and that accordingly the authority to use force under resolution 678 had revived and continued to that date. He ended: 'Resolution 1441 would in terms have provided that a further decision of the Security Council to sanction force was required if that had been intended. Thus, all that Resolution 1441 requires is reporting to and discussion by the Security Council of Iraq's failures, but not an express further decision to authorise force.'

This statement was, I think, flawed in two fundamental respects. First, it was not plain that Iraq had failed to comply in a manner justifying resort to force and there were no strong factual grounds or hard evidence to show that it had: Hans Blix and his team of weapons inspectors had found no weapons of mass destruction, were making progress and expected to complete their task in a matter of months. Secondly, it cannot be accepted that a determination whether Iraq had failed to avail itself of its final opportunity was intended to be taken otherwise than collectively by the Security Council. The revival argument itself has been ill-received. Lord Alexander of Weedon QC in his brilliant Tom Sargant memorial annual lecture for JUSTICE of 14 October 2003 (without access to the Attorney General's earlier advice) described it as 'unconvincing'.[39] Professor Sands QC has called it 'a bad argument'.[40] Professor Lowe has described the argument as 'fatuous': 'The whole point of the UN system is that when the Security Council is seised of a problem it is the Council, and not individual Member States, that has the right to control matters. If the Security Council had intended that the United States, the United Kingdom and others should invade Iraq in 2003 with its blessing and its mandate, it would have said so. It did not.'[41]

If I am right that the invasion of Iraq by the US, the UK and some other states was unauthorized by the Security Council there was, of course, a serious violation of international law and of the rule of law. For the effect of acting unilaterally was to undermine the foundation on which the post-1945 consensus had been constructed: the prohibition of force (save in self-defence, or, perhaps, to avert an impending humanitarian catastrophe) unless formally authorized by the nations of the world empowered to make collective decisions in the Security Council under Chapter VII of the UN Charter. The moment that a state treats the rules of international law as binding on others but not on itself, the compact on which the law rests is broken. 'It is', as has been said, 'the difference between the role of world policeman and world vigilante.'[42]

I should make it plain that Mr Jack Straw, Foreign Secretary in March 2003, and Lord Goldsmith, Attorney General at the time, strongly challenge the conclusions I have expressed,[43] and others may also do so.

Lord Goldsmith has emphasized that he believed the advice which he gave at the time to be correct – which I have not challenged – and remains of that view. On the issue of legality he has stressed three points in particular. First, the use of force in 2003 was (he has said) authorized by the United Nations because of the original authorization, which remained in force. He has pointed out that the revival argument had been relied on before, had been consistently supported by British Law Officers and had been endorsed by the Secretary-General of the UN in 1993 and by the then Legal Advisor to the UN. Resolution 678 was not tied to expelling Iraq from Kuwait.

His second point is that the Security Council did set the conditions for the permission to use force to revive. Resolution 1441 made a finding of material breach and gave Iraq a final opportunity to comply. This did not require the Security Council to decide that there had been a further material breach. The negotiating history made this clear.

His third point is that the UK was justified in concluding that the final opportunity had not been taken. He had advised the Prime Minister that he had to be sure. Resolution 1441 was not about weapons of mass destruction. Under resolution 1441 Iraq had to co-operate fully and the British government judged that it had not done so.

Mr Straw has agreed with what Lord Goldsmith has said. The negotiating history and wording of resolution 1441 show, he has said, that it was not the intention of the Security Council, nor was it so expressed, that a decision on material breach had to be decided by the Security Council. This might be surprising, he comments, but it is true.

The question, then, is one of authority. This suggests three questions calling for an answer. First, who was authorized? Resolution 678 authorized 'the Member States cooperating with the Government of Kuwait'. That expression had a very clear meaning in 1991. But it could scarcely be read as a reference to a shrunken core of two of the former coalition partners, shorn of most of their former partners and against the strong vocal opposition of several of them. The multilateral application of resolution 678 was an important feature of it.

The second question is: what did resolution 678 give authority to do? The answer is clear. It gave authority to expel Iraq from Kuwait and 'restore peace and security in the area'. It is difficult to read this as authority to launch a full-scale invasion of Iraq in 2003 with the obvious intention of depositing its government and occupying its territory, the foreseeable consequence of causing widespread loss of life, and the potential to destabilize the area.

The third question is: when was authority given to invade? It cannot be plausibly suggested that authority was given by resolution 1441, for that gave the Iraqi government a final opportunity to co-operate. Clearly, therefore, an invasion could not have been launched the next day. But if not then, when? As soon as any member state of the UN decided that the Iraqi government had had sufficient time to co-operate and had not done so? This, as I have already suggested, would subvert the collective decision-making process of the Security Council which lies at the heart of the Chapter VII regime. A decision as massive and far-reaching as one to invade and occupy a foreign sovereign state must be based on something very much more solid than a good arguable case. The inescapable truth is that the British government wished and tried to obtain a further Security Council resolution authorizing the use of force, but was unable to do so in the face of international opposition and went ahead without.

The legal duties of belligerents while hostilities are in progress and after they have ended are very largely governed by the regulations annexed to the 1907 Hague Convention and by the four 1949 Geneva Conventions as extended by Protocols adopted in 1977. These give effect to a wide international consensus that there are some methods of making war which are impermissible (such as killing or wounding an enemy who is already wounded or has surrendered, and the destruction of property without military necessity); that prisoners of war should be protected, and treated with humanity and decency; and that civilians, non-combatants, the sick and the wounded should be so far as possible protected from the military activity. When hostilities are over, an occupying power 'shall take all measures in [its] power to restore, and ensure, as far as possible, public order and safety, while respecting, unless absolutely prevented, the laws in force in the country'.[44] Property and life must be respected.[45] The occupying power has no mandate to transform the law and institutions of the defeated state, a somewhat anomalous rule given that the two most successful post-1945 occupations, those of West Germany and Japan, comprehensively transformed the laws and institutions of those countries.[46]

The record of the British as an occupying power in Iraq has, as we know, been sullied by a number of incidents, most notably the shameful beating to death of Mr Baha Mousa in Basra.[47] But such breaches of the law were not a result of deliberate government policy, and the rights of the victims have been recognized. This contrasts with the unilateral decisions of the US government that the Geneva Conventions did not apply to the detention conditions in Guantanamo Bay, Cuba, or to trial of Al-Qaeda or Taleban prisoners by military commissions,[48] that Al-Qaeda suspects should be denied the rights of both prisoners of war and criminal suspects, and that torture should be redefined, contrary to the Torture Convention and the consensus of international opinion, to connote pain, where physical, 'of an intensity akin to that which accompanies serious physical injury such as death or organ failure'.[49] This is what underlay the abuses indelibly associated in the mind of the world with the photographs of Abu Ghraib but occurring elsewhere also, described in horrifying detail in reports of the International Committee of the Red Cross (February 2004 and February 2007),[50] General Taguba (March 2004),[51] Generals Fay and Jones (August 2004 and February 2007)[52] and the American Bar Association (August 2004).[53] Particularly disturbing to proponents of the rule of law is the cynical lack of concern for international legality among some top officials in the Bush administration. Thus in one memorandum the Deputy Assistant Attorney General (John Yoo), writing to the Counsel to the President, advised:

Thus we conclude that the Bush administration's understanding created a valid and effective reservation to the Torture Convention. Even if it were otherwise, there is no international court to review the conduct of the United States under the Convention. In an additional reservation, the United States refused to accept the jurisdiction of the [International Court of Justice] (which, in any event, could hear only a case brought by another state, not by an individual) to adjudicate cases under the Convention. Although the Convention creates a Committee to monitor compliance, it can only conduct studies and has no enforcement powers.[54]

The British government did not adopt practices such as these, of which a number of prominent British ministers (including the Attorney General) were openly critical.

As I stressed at the outset, most transactions governed by international law proceed smoothly and routinely on the strength of known and accepted rules. I have perhaps dwelt disproportionately on the non-compliant tip of the iceberg, illustrated by events in Iraq and elsewhere. But those events highlight what seem to me to be the two most serious deficiencies of the rule of law in the international order. The first is the willingness of some states in some circumstances to rewrite the rules to meet the perceived exigencies of the political situation, as the UK did in relation to the Suez crisis of 1956. The second is the consensual basis of the jurisdiction of the International Court of Justice (ICJ). Cases come before the Court only if the parties agree. While 65 of the 192 member states of the United Nations have chosen to accept the compulsory jurisdiction of the ICJ, a majority do not, and it is a lamentable fact that, of the five permanent members of the Security Council, only one, the UK, now does so, Russia and China never having done so and France and the United States having withdrawn earlier acceptances. As HE Judge Rosalyn Higgins, then the President of the ICJ, said in a lecture at the British Institute of International and Comparative Law in October 2007, 'the absence of a compulsory recourse to the Court falls short of a recognisable "rule of law" model'.[55] The suggestion that the rule of law requires, in this day and age, a routine and obligatory recourse to the Court in matters connected to the UN Charter and related issues is obviously, she suggested, still a step too far. But it is, I think, a step which must be taken if the rule of law is to become truly effective in this area.

If events in Iraq and elsewhere highlight some of the deficiencies of international law, they may nonetheless yield a public benefit in the longer term. For while the lawfulness of earlier military interventions has attracted academic analysis (as, notably, by Geoffrey Marston on the Suez crisis[56]), I do not think the public at large has been much interested in whether the interventions were lawful or not. In the case of Iraq, perhaps because of widespread doubt in this country about the wisdom and necessity of going to war, the issue of legality has loomed larger than, I think, ever before. This has enhanced the importance of international law in the public mind, and Chapter VII of the UN Charter has come to be more widely recognized not only as a constraint on unauthorized military action but also as a guarantee that such action is necessary to maintain or restore peace and proportionate, traditional conditions of a just war. While prophecy is always perilous, it is perhaps unlikely that states chastened by their experience in Iraq will be eager to repeat it. They have not been hauled before the ICJ or any other tribunal to answer for their actions, but they have been arraigned at the bar of world opinion, and judged unfavourably, with resulting damage to their standing and influence. If the daunting challenges now facing the world are to be overcome, it must be in important part through the medium of rules, internationally agreed, internationally implemented and, if necessary, internationally enforced. That is what the rule of law requires in the international order.[57]

PART III

II

Terrorism and the Rule of Law

[T]he United States will not support any and all measures taken in the name of fighting drugs and all measures taken in the name of fighting drugs and terrorism or restoring stability. One of the most dangerous temptations for a government facing violent threats is to respond in heavy-handed ways that violate the rights of innocent citizens. Terrorism is a criminal act and should be treated accordingly – and that means applying the law fairly and consistently. We have found, through experience round the world, that the best way to defeat terrorist threats is to increase law enforcement capabilities while at the same time promoting democracy and human rights.

The speaker was Madeleine Albright, the US Secretary of State, the date 17 April 2000, the occasion a speech to the University of World Economy and Diplomacy at Tashkent in Uzbekistan.

History does not, so far as I know, record how the Uzbeks reacted to the Secretary of State's remarks, but they would at the time have struck an American audience as orthodox, consistent with the rule of law and reflective of the values which the United States prides itself on observing. Many Americans would have looked back with a sense of shame and regret to occasions when the United States had overreacted to a perceived threat, as in the round-up of supposed anarchists after the First World War, the detention of 110,000 Japanese Americans after Pearl Harbor, the effective kidnapping of 2,264 Japanese from Central America (also after Pearl Harbor) and the persecution of suspected Communists instigated by Senator McCarthy. Very many Americans would have recognized the truth of what Supreme Court Justice William Brennan had said in 1987:

There is considerably less to be proud about, and a good deal to be embarrassed about, when one reflects on the shabby treatment civil liberties have received in the United States during times of war and perceived threats to national security ... After each perceived security crisis ended, the United States has remorsefully realized that the abrogation of civil liberties was unnecessary. But it has proven unable to prevent itself from repeating the error when the next crisis came along.[1]

In Britain, the Secretary of State's remarks would have raised no eyebrows. Britain had experienced spasmodic outbursts of terrorist violence (or attempted violence) at home since at least the time of Guy Fawkes, had responded with force (and on occasion brutality) to emergencies in various parts of the empire and had detained enemy aliens during two world wars. It had also, very recently, endured three decades of extreme terrorist violence, both in Northern Ireland and on the mainland of Britain. This traumatic experience was important in two respects particularly. First, it was important because the British government had throughout treated terrorism as a civil emergency, not a war, and had treated the terrorists, republican or loyalist, as criminals and not as combatants. It was important, secondly, because the British authorities, having resorted to internment of those suspected of involvement in terrorism and to methods of interrogation condemned at Strasbourg as inhuman and degrading treatment,[2] abandoned these methods as ineffective and counter-productive, alienating the very people on whose support the stability of the state depended.

The events which took place in New York, Washington and Pennsylvania on 11 September 2001 are too well known to call for recapitulation here. I shall refer to them compendiously as '9/11'. They traumatized the American people and shocked the world. In the United States, and also in Britain (which suffered its own, smaller and less lethal, attack on 7 July 2005), the authorities reappraised the orthodox approach described by Madeleine Albright.

In the United States, the Attorney General, John Ashcroft, announced: 'In order to fight and defeat terrorism, the Department of Justice has added a new paradigm to that of prosecution – a paradigm of prevention.'[3] This new paradigm seems, at first blush, to have much to commend it. Prevention is better than cure. Better, surely, to try to prevent a further attack occurring than to wait for another attack and then try to catch any of the perpetrators who might still be alive. The loyal and law-abiding would have nothing to fear. President George W. Bush, in his State of the Union address in January 2002, had declared, to applause, that: 'America will always stand firm for the non-negotiable demands of human dignity; the rule of law; limits on the power of the state; respect for women; private property; free speech; equal justice; and religious tolerance.' Justice Hugo Black of the US Supreme Court had in 1964 described the United States as 'dedicated' to the rule of law.[4]

But Arthur Chaskalson, a greatly respected Chief Justice of South Africa in post-apartheid times, has drawn a parallel between the behaviour of the 1950s governments of South Africa and that of the Bush administration:

The initial steps taken in South Africa in the 1950s laid the ground for further measures including the banning of the African National Congress, the Pan African Congress and over time various other anti-apartheid organizations [98 in all], and the draconian security legislation of the 1960s and later years. Political rhetoric set the scene for this and for the legislation that followed. The white voters were warned that the state was facing a total onslaught. They were told that the legislation was not directed against law-abiding citizens and would not affect them. The targets were the communists and the terrorists. The great majority of the white population remained silent and there was little opposition to the measures. Detention without trial was introduced, the police were empowered to hold detainees incommunicado, and to deny them access to their lawyers or their own medical advisors. Initially detention was for 90 days, then for 180 days and then indefinitely. Courts were stripped of their jurisdiction to make habeas corpus orders in respect of detainees. The isolation of the detainees and the ousting of the jurisdiction of the courts led to torture and other abuses, which have been documented in the hearings of the Truth and Reconciliation Commission.[5]

On the international plane, the Bush administration's rejection of an approach consistent with the rule of law was express. In 2005 the

Pentagon, in its National Defense Strategy, warned that 'Our strength as a nation state will continue to be challenged by those who employ a strategy of the weak, using international fora, judicial processes, and terrorism.'[6] As a not unsympathetic American author, writing in 2004, observed, 'One may safely conclude that the current US administration is no fan of the collective security approach enshrined in the UN Charter.'[7]

In Britain also the mood music changed. This was reflected in the then Prime Minister Tony Blair's observation at his monthly press conference on 5 August 2005, after the July bombings, when he said: 'Let no one be in any doubt, the rules of the game are changing . . .' This was not, perhaps, a happy choice of phrase, since no responsible person had ever supposed there was a game. A learned author, having examined the matter at length, has concluded that the only rule-change has been found in the greater willingness of the courts to uphold civil liberties and hold the government to account for its breaches of the law.[8] But Mr Blair can at least claim the virtue of consistency. On the point of leaving office, in an article published on 27 May 2007,[9] he described it as a 'dangerous misjudgment' to put civil liberties first. To do so was, he said, 'misguided and wrong'. While neither he nor other ministers have, I think, quoted Cicero directly, their guiding principle has been Cicero's phrase 'Salus populi suprema est lex' (the safety of the people is the supreme law); in his foreword to 'The UK's Strategy for Countering International Terrorism', published in March 2009, the Prime Minister, Mr Gordon Brown, paraphrased Cicero when he said: 'The first priority of any Government is to ensure the security and safety of the nation and all members of the public.' This is a view which many support, in Britain and the United States.[10] But John Selden (1584–1654), who did not lack experience of civil strife, observed 'There is not any thing in the world more abused than this sentence.'[11] A preferable view to Cicero's, perhaps, is that attributed to Benjamin Franklin, that 'he who would put security before liberty deserves neither'.[12] We cannot commend our society to others by departing from the fundamental standards which make it worthy of commendation.

The war on terror

In some ways, the response of the US and British governments to the potent threat of Al-Qaeda terrorism has been markedly different. I draw attention to three important differences (and others could doubtless be added). First, the President of the United States very publicly declared a 'War on Terror'. This was no doubt in part a politician's rhetorical flourish, comparable with declaring war on want, or poverty, or drugs, or HIV AIDS. But it was not only a rhetorical flourish. It had substantive consequences also. For once a terrorist or potential terrorist was viewed as an enemy rather than a criminal suspect, it followed that his status was governed by the law of armed conflict (if any law at all) rather than the criminal law, difficult questions were bound to (and duly did) arise on the applicability of the third Geneva Convention of 1949, and the United States found itself committed to a war of indefinite duration against an ill-defined enemy on a worldwide battlefield. Professor Conor Gearty has described 'the supersession of the criminal model based on justice and due process by a security model that is based on fear and suspicion' as 'the single greatest disastrous legacy of the war on terror from a human rights point of view'.[13] The British, by contrast, adhered to the course established in Northern Ireland of treating terrorists as criminals, not combatants. This may be why the British authorities have been more successful than their American counterparts in prosecuting terrorists to conviction, as suggested by Professor David Cole of Georgetown University in an article entitled 'The Brits Do It Better'.[14] He pointed out that the British response to terrorism had been 'considerably more restrained and sensitive to rights', 'more measured, nuanced and carefully tailored' than that of the United States and quoted with approval a statement by the Director of Public Prosecutions, Sir Ken Macdonald QC: 'the fight against terrorism on the streets of Britain is not a war. It is the prevention of crime ... a culture of legislative restraint in the area of terrorist crime is central to the existence of an efficient and human-rights compatible process.' This restraint may, Professor Cole considered, have contributed to the UK's apparently greater success at disrupting terrorist plots and bringing terrorists to justice.

Executive power

The second difference flows from the first. By a resolution adopted on 18 September 2001 the US Congress authorized the President to

use all necessary and appropriate force against those nations, organizations, or persons he determines planned, authorized, committed, or aided the terrorist attacks that occurred on September 11, 2001, or harbored such organizations or persons, in order to prevent any future acts of international terrorism against the United States by such nations, organizations or persons.

This was followed on 13 November 2001 by a Presidential Military Order which aimed to 'identify terrorists and those who support them, to disrupt their activities, and to eliminate their ability to conduct or support [terrorist] attacks [and for suspects] to be detained, and, when tried, to be tried ... by military tribunals'.[15] The Order applied to individuals who were not US citizens and who were or had been, or had knowingly harboured, a member of Al-Qaeda or had engaged in, aided or abetted, or conspired to commit, acts of international terrorism prejudicial to the interest of the United States. It authorized the detention of suspects at any designated location worldwide with no guarantee of trial. It prescribed that suspects, if tried, would be tried by a military commission, with standards of evidence lower than those applicable in the ordinary courts and with power to impose the death penalty.[16] Even if the United States had been engaged in a major war, these were immense powers to confer on the executive, empowering the President to use force against any person or entity he might determine to be responsible, and providing for the indefinite detention of suspected terrorists anywhere in the world without any guarantee of charge or trial. The Westminster Parliament conferred no comparable powers on the executive in Britain.

Extraordinary rendition

A third difference between the UK and US responses to Al-Qaeda terrorism relates to the practice of rendition, a new expression originally used to describe the unlawful seizing (in effect, kidnapping) of a person in one country in order to remove him to stand trial in another country. The British courts had experience of such a case in 1993 and the House of Lords held that the courts should refuse to try a defendant brought to this country in flagrant breach of international law.[17] That decision was followed by the Court of Appeal in a case concerning an IRA terrorist who was unlawfully abducted in Zimbabwe, brought to this country, charged, fairly tried and convicted. His eventual appeal was allowed because the conduct of the authorities was a blatant and extremely serious failure to adhere to the rule of law with regard to the production of a defendant for prosecution in the English courts.[18]

The American approach is rather different.[19] If a defendant is duly indicted in an American court, the court will not enquire how he came to be in the country at all. Three defendants were, it seems, rendered to the United States to stand trial in the decade before 1995,[20] but in that year President Clinton issued a Presidential Decision Directive which stated: 'where we do not receive adequate cooperation from a State that harbors a terrorist whose extradition we are seeking, we shall take appropriate measures to induce cooperation. Return of suspects by force may be effected without the cooperation of the host government.'[21] This led to a steep increase in the number of renditions: forty in the three years following the Directive.[22] But in all these cases the suspect was seized in order that he should stand trial in the United States. After September 2001 the practice was altered and has been called 'extraordinary rendition'. This involved the seizure of a suspect and his removal to a third country where he would suffer ill-treatment or torture with the object, not of putting him on trial, but of extracting information from him. Three cases, the facts of which have not, to my knowledge, been challenged, illustrate the operation of extraordinary rendition in practice.

Mr El-Masri, a German citizen, claimed that he went to Macedonia on holiday. After entering, he was detained by Macedonian officials, who handed him over to CIA operatives. They took him to a CIA-operated detention centre near Kabul, where he was held incommunicado for some months, beaten, drugged and mistreated in other ways. After about five months he was released in a remote area of Albania, from which he made his way back to Germany. He brought an action against the CIA in the United States, claiming damages for his kidnapping and mistreatment. But the Federal District Court (affirmed by the Court of Appeals) dismissed his claim, without any hearing of the merits, on the ground that it could not be tried without revealing state secrets concerning the operations of the CIA, and the Supreme Court declined to entertain an appeal.[23] It appears that Mr El-Masri may have been picked up because his name resembled that of an associate of one of the 9/11 hijackers, and that his release was ordered by the Secretary of State when the mistake of identity was appreciated.[24]

Mr Maher Arar, although born in Syria, was a citizen of Canada, where he had lived and worked for seventeen years. In September 2002 he interrupted a holiday in Tunisia because he was called back to Canada by his employers. On his way home he passed through John F. Kennedy airport in New York. There he was arrested by the US authorities in reliance on information given them by the Canadian police. He was not advised of his right to consular access, and the Canadian authorities were not told that he was in US custody. He was held in the United States for twelve days, then rendered to Jordan, then rendered to Syria, where he was imprisoned, tortured and held in degrading and inhuman conditions for a year. At the end of that period the Syrians released him, and he returned to Canada – not passing through JFK. Like Mr El-Masri, he brought an action against the American authorities, but this was dismissed on much the same grounds as Mr El-Masri's. The Canadian government was, however, stung into establishing a judicial inquiry into the case. After two and a half years of investigation Justice O'Connor found that Mr Arar was innocent of wrong-doing; that he was an innocent victim of US, Syrian and Canadian officials; that the Canadian authorities had given false and misleading information to their American counterparts; and that the US State Department was aware that Syria routinely tortured its detainees. The judge's recommendations led to a public apology by the Prime Minister of Canada, the resignation of the commissioner of police and the payment of compensation in the sum of $Can10 million.[25]

The cases of Mr Bisher Al-Rawi and Mr Jamil El-Banna brought home to the British authorities that individuals wholly unconnected with the conflict in Afghanistan might be the subject of extraordinary rendition and that, if information was given to the US authorities subject to a caveat or condition as to how it should be used, reliance could not be placed on American observance of the condition. The story is told in the report on *Rendition* made by the Intelligence and Security Committee of the House of Commons in July 2007.[26]

Mr Al-Rawi was an Iraqi national who had lived in Britain since 1984. He had been granted exceptional leave to remain, but had not applied for UK citizenship. Mr El-Banna was a Jordanian-Palestinian, recognized as a refugee in Britain but not a citizen. The two men had attracted the attention of the Security Service and were believed to be associated with Abu Qatada, a radical cleric. At the end of October 2002 the Security Service made an attempt, apparently unsuccessfully, to seek the co-operation of Mr El-Banna. On 1 November 2002 the two men, with another (a UK citizen), arrived at Gatwick airport to fly to Gambia, on, they said, business. A covert search was made of their baggage and an item was found in Mr Al-Rawi's luggage which was thought to be suspicious. All three men were arrested. The Security Service reported the arrest and their assessment of the men to the US authorities in a telegram which made clear that the information was for 'research and analysis purposes only and may not be used as the basis for overt, covert or executive action'. The three men were questioned between 1 and 4 November, and their homes searched. But it would seem that nothing incriminating was found, since it was judged that there was insufficient evidence on which to charge the men, and they were released on 4 November. The US authorities were informed, as also that the men were expected to travel to Gambia shortly. They were asked to pass on this information to the Gambians, and to ascertain whether the Gambians could 'cover these individuals whilst they are in Gambia'. This telegram also contained a condition prohibiting 'overt, covert or executive action', which was expected to be passed on to the Gambians. Thus no arrest was intended or contemplated.

On 8 November 2002 the three men returned to Gatwick and flew to Gambia. Details of the flight were passed to the Americans. On arrival at Banjul, the men were greeted by a Gambian national and Mr Al-Rawi's brother, a UK national. The Gambian authorities searched the travellers' luggage, found items regarded as suspicious and arrested all five men. The Gambian national was released the next day. The arrests were reported to the Security Service on 10 November.

The four remaining men were initially detained by the Gambian authorities, and later by the Americans. The Security Service were told about the progress of the investigation, but not of the men's whereabouts.

In late November the Security Service were informed by the US authorities that the four men were to be removed to Bagram Air Base in Afghanistan. They registered concerns, orally and in writing. Strong representations were made to the US ambassador in Banjul and to the State Department and the National Security Council in Washington. To no avail. The US authorities declined to reveal where the men were, and denied consular access to the two UK nationals, in clear breach of the Vienna Convention on Consular Relations. The UK nationals were released and returned to the UK on 4 and 5 December 2002, leaving Mr Al-Rawi and Mr El-Banna in American hands. The Security Service assured the Americans that the British government would not seek to extend consular protection to them.

Mr Al-Rawi and Mr El-Banna were taken to Bagram Air Base by the US authorities on 8 December. After a period in custody there, they were detained in Kabul before transfer, in February 2003, to Guantanamo Bay, where, as the British courts later assumed, they suffered mistreatment that was, at least, inhuman and degrading. At Guantanamo Bay, Combatant Status Review Tribunals, whose function was to determine whether detainees were enemy combatants, found that they both were, and both were properly detained. After just over four years' detention at Guantanamo, they were released and returned to the UK in March 2007. Their release followed representations by the Foreign and Commonwealth Office, perhaps prompted by the suggestion that Mr Al-Rawi had formerly worked, or would if released work, for the Security Service, and also followed an action brought by him in the High Court in London.[27] He has been charged with no offence.

The Intelligence and Security Committee expressed its conclusion in this way:

What the rendition programme has shown is that in what it refers to as 'the war on terror' the US will take whatever action it deems necessary, within US law, to protect its national security from those it considers to pose a serious threat. Although the US may take note of UK protests and concerns, this does not appear materially to affect its strategy on rendition.[28]

In its Response to this Report the Government referred to assurances by the US Secretary of State that the United States respected the sovereignty of other countries and did not transport detainees to other countries for the purposes of interrogation using torture.[29] But the Committee might have added that in what it refers to as 'the war on terror' the United States would take whatever action it deems necessary to protect its national interest from those it considers to pose a serious threat, in disregard of international and international human rights law. On present information, the British government is not shown to have been complicit in the US programme of extraordinary rendition, and even the full extent of its knowledge has not been established. There appears in this respect to have been an important difference in the response of the two countries to the threat of terrorism, but the full facts have yet to emerge.

Legislation

So much for the differences between the US and UK responses to 9/11. What of the similarities? Again, there are a number. I shall refer to seven.

First, both countries responded to the threat by legislation. In the United States this took the form of the artfully named Uniting and Strengthening America by Providing Appropriate Tools Required to Intercept and Obstruct Terrorism Act 2001, abbreviated to the USA PATRIOT Act. This was a very substantial measure, containing 134 provisions and covering 342 pages. It was rushed through both Houses of Congress with little debate, very limited public hearings, and without a conference or committee report. In the UK the pattern was rather similar, although more surprising, since following years of experience of terrorism in Northern Ireland and much deliberation Parliament had as recently as the year 2000 enacted a comprehensive Terrorism Act running to 131 sections and 16 schedules. But following the attacks on

11 September it enacted, within a very short period, the Anti-terrorism, Crime and Security Act 2001. Parliament has not, however, rested on its laurels. Since the 2001 Act it has passed no fewer than five further Acts amending or adding to the law on terrorism.

Non-nationals

Secondly, the anti-terrorist legislation of both countries has in the first instance directed many of the most stringent provisions against those who were not citizens and who therefore had no absolute right to remain in the country. In the PATRIOT Act, terrorism was defined in one sense for domestic purposes and another, much broader, sense for immigration purposes. As Professor Cole has written:

Neither Congress nor the executive branch made any attempt to explain why the same act should be 'terrorist' when committed by a foreign national but not when committed by a US citizen. This differential treatment runs throughout the PATRIOT Act, which reserves its most severe measures for noncitizens. It makes foreign nationals deportable for wholly innocent associational activity, excludable for pure speech, and subject to incarceration on the attorney-general's say so, without a finding that they pose a danger or a flight risk. A provision that applies largely but not exclusively to foreign nationals authorizes secret searches in criminal investigations without probable cause of criminal activity, the constitutional minimum for criminal searches. With a stroke of the pen, in other words, President Bush denied foreign nationals basic rights of political association, political speech, due process, and privacy.[30]

The centrepiece of the PATRIOT Act's immigration provisions rendered non-citizens liable to deportation for their associations with disfavoured organizations.

Discrimination against non-citizens was, it appears, deliberate administration policy. As Professors Cole and Lobel have written:

When Attorney General John Ashcroft first announced 'the paradigm of prevention' in a speech in October 2001 in New York City, he vowed that the administration would use all laws within its power to round up suspected terrorists and prevent them from inflicting further damage upon us. He explicitly singled out immigration law, warning terrorists that if they 'over-stayed [their] visa by even one day' they would be locked up. The administration subsequently adopted a zero-tolerance immigration policy toward immigrants and visitors from Arab and Muslim countries, on the theory that it would thereby root out the terrorists. But the nation's broadest campaign of ethnic profiling since World War II came up empty. The Special Registration program, which required 80,000 men from predominantly Arab and Muslim countries to register after September 11, resulted in not a single terrorist conviction. Of the 8,000 young men of Arab and Muslim descent sought out for FBI interviews, and the more than 5,000 foreign nationals placed in preventive detention in the first two years after 9/11, virtually all Arab and Muslim, not one stands convicted of a terrorist crime today. In these initiatives, this government's record is 0 for 93,000.[31]

This discriminatory approach was mirrored in Part 4 of the Anti-terrorism, Crime and Security Act 2001, which provided for the indef-inite detention without charge or trial of foreign nationals suspected of involvement in terrorism, but not of UK citizens who might be (and in fact were) similarly suspected of involvement in terrorism. Such dis-crimination was, again, a deliberate political decision, as explained by the then Home Secretary (David Blunkett) in a discussion paper (already quoted in Chapter 5): 'While it would be possible to seek other powers to detain British citizens who may be involved in interna-tional terrorism it would be a very grave step. The Government believes that such draconian powers would be difficult to justify . . .'.[32]

Detention without charge or trial

The third similarity lies in the resort of both countries, although on a very different scale, to the practice just mentioned of detaining suspects indefinitely without charge or trial, a practice formerly regarded as the hallmark of repressive authoritarian regimes. In the United States the government's preventive detention programme, largely directed (as already noted) at Arabs and Muslims, led to the detention of 1,182 people in the first seven weeks of the programme[33] and ultimately to the detention of about 5,000,[34] many of them on no charge at all, on the strength of vague, anonymous accusations. Very few have been convicted of terrorism. The United States has also authorized and carried out disappearances of alleged Al-Qaeda members into secret prisons and conducted mass round-ups and secret arrests at home and abroad. It has claimed and exercised the right to detain without charge or trial anyone the President chooses to designate as an enemy combatant.[35] The number of people rounded up and detained in Afghanistan, Iraq and other unidentified 'black' sites around the world is not known, but the Pentagon is said to have conceded that the United States has detained more than 80,000 people,[36] of whom nearly 800 were held for a time at Guantanamo Bay.[37] Some of these were as young as thirteen,[38] and there were very few terrorists among them.[39]

The Bush administration's practice of detaining foreign terrorist suspects at Guantanamo Bay led to a series of three decisions in the Supreme Court of the United States, all of them adverse to the administration. In the first of these cases (*Rasul v Bush*),[40] the issue was whether a non-citizen detainee had a statutory right to challenge his detention in a US court. A majority held that he had. Citing Magna Carta, Stevens J (for the majority) ruled: 'Executive imprisonment has been considered oppressive and lawless since King John at Runnymede pledged that no free man should be imprisoned, dispossessed, outlawed or exiled save by the judgment of his peers or by the law of the land'. Thus Mr Rasul was entitled to claim habeas corpus in the civilian courts.

Following a legislative change, made to deprive the detainees of the benefit of this decision, the second case came before the court: *Hamdan v Rumsfeld*.[41] In this case, a majority held that the legislation did not prevent federal courts hearing habeas corpus petitions already pending, that detainees were entitled to the protection of common Article 3 of the Geneva Conventions (which prohibits cruel treatment and torture) and that detainees were entitled, if tried, to trial before 'a regularly constituted court affording all the judicial guarantees recognized as indispensable by civilized peoples'.

Following a further legislative change, and after an unusual procedural twist well described by Tim Otty QC (who was part of a team which made submissions in all three of these cases),[42] the third case reached the Supreme Court: *Boumediene v Bush*.[43] Again, the decision was by a majority. It was a decisive defeat for the administration. The majority held that the detainees had a constitutional right to habeas corpus, that the legislation purporting to remove that right was unconstitutional and that trial in the tribunals established to determine the status of the detainees was no substitute for habeas corpus, lacking important procedural safeguards. Kennedy J, giving judgment for the majority, cited Magna Carta, the *Five Knights' Case* (leading to the Petition of Right) and the case of James Somerset. He also cited Alexander Hamilton's observation, during the debate on the US Constitution, that 'The practice of arbitrary imprisonment has been in all ages the favourite and most formidable instrument of tyranny.' He concluded: 'The laws and Constitution are designed to survive, and remain in force in extraordinary times. Liberty and security can be reconciled; and in our system they are reconciled within the law.' Thus it may be said that, in the end, the rule of law was vindicated. But not before the detainees had undergone long years of unlawful imprisonment and suffered much ill-treatment.

The UK response was on a much more modest scale, and was initially directed to a particular group of people: foreign nationals with no right to live in the UK, who were suspected of involvement in terrorism, but who could not be deported to their home countries. In the ordinary way, the Home Secretary may deport a foreign national whose presence in this country is judged not to be conducive to the public good, as would be so in the case of a person suspected of involvement in terrorism. Pending deportation a person may be detained in custody, but only for a reasonable time, not indefinitely.[44] The problem facing the British government was twofold: under Article 5 of the European Convention on Human Rights (discussed in Chapter 7) a prospective deportee might only be detained pending deportation and might not be detained if no deportation was in prospect; but a decision of the European Court, binding on the UK, forbade the deportation of a person to his home country, even if he was thought to be a risk to national security, if he ran a real risk of being tortured in that country. Such was the decision made in *Chahal v United Kingdom*:[45]

Mr Chahal was a Sikh separatist living in the UK, suspected of terrorism in his native India and at risk of torture by Punjabi forces if deported to his homeland. How, then, was the UK to tackle the problem posed by foreign nationals suspected of involvement in terrorism who could not be deported to their home countries in the Middle East and North Africa because of the risk of torture on their return, and who, since they could not be deported, could not be detained pending deportation?

The solution adopted by the British government, with the blessing of Parliament, was to derogate from (in effect, opt out of) Article 5 of the Convention. This is a power which may be exercised in relation to some (but not all) articles of the Convention if certain conditions are fulfilled. The conditions are laid down in Article 15 of the Convention and apply '[i]n time of war or other public emergency threatening the life of the nation', but the opt-out may only be 'to the extent strictly required by the exigencies of the situation' and provided that the measures taken 'are not inconsistent with [the state's] other obligations under international law'. The government judged that the conditions were fulfilled, and opted out of Article 5 so as to permit the detention of foreign nationals suspected of involvement in terrorism even where, because of the decision in *Chahal*, they could not be deported.

The power to detain foreign nationals under Part 4 was exercised in sixteen cases.[46] In what came to be known as 'the *Belmarsh* case',[47] briefly mentioned in Chapters 5 and 7 above, nine of those detained, held in high security conditions at Belmarsh Prison, issued proceedings challenging the lawfulness of their detention. They argued that the conditions for opting out of Article 5 were not met, and that even if they were the legislation was incompatible with the UK's obligations under the European Convention. The action wound its way up the hierarchy of courts but they were unsuccessful in the Court of Appeal and in October 2004 their appeal came before an enlarged court of nine Law Lords in the House of Lords. They gave judgment on 15 December 2004. One of the Law Lords ruled that the conditions for opting out of Article 5 were not met, since even an outrage like that of 9/11 did not threaten the life of the British nation, but the others, with varying degrees of enthusiasm, held that the question involved a political judgment with which they should not interfere. On the main question, the Law Lords ruled, by a majority of 7 to 1, that Part 4 was incompatible with the UK's obligations under the Convention. They held that the measure did not rationally address the threat to security, was not a proportionate response, was not strictly required by the exigencies of the situation and unjustifiably discriminated against foreign nationals on grounds of their nationality.

The Law Lords' conclusion did not oblige Parliament or the government to repeal or amend Part 4. There was a choice: to maintain Part 4, and run the risk of defeat by the appellants in Strasbourg; or to substitute an alternative regime. The latter course was chosen. As briefly mentioned in Chapter 9, the Prevention of Terrorism Act 2005 provided for the making by the Home Secretary (subject to review by the High Court) of control orders against persons whom he reasonably suspected of involvement in terrorism-related activity if he considered it necessary to impose obligations on such persons for protecting the public against terrorism. The obligations which such orders could impose could place very severe restrictions on those subject to them, confining them to an allocated flat in an unfamiliar place for long hours each day, restricting whom they might meet, denying them ordinary means of communication, obliging them to wear an electronic tag, rendering them liable to be searched by the authorities at any time of day or night, and exposing them to the risk of imprisonment for up to five years if any condition of the order was breached. But the orders were called 'non-derogating control orders' because they could not, if made by the Home Secretary, deprive a person of his liberty in a way which would infringe Article 5: to do so would require the UK, again, to opt out of Article 5, an exercise which was not repeated after the judgment in the *Belmarsh* case. Eighteen such orders have been made,[48] and again there was a challenge to the lawfulness of the legislation on a number of grounds, among them that the conditions imposed did, cumulatively, deprive those subject to them of their liberty. When the case reached the House of Lords in 2007, a majority of Law Lords held that the restrictions in one case, which included an eighteen-hour curfew, did, cumulatively, deprive the subject of his liberty.[49] But shorter curfews (for ten or twelve hours per day) and less rigorous restrictions were held in other cases to be compatible with Article 5[50] and the Law

Lords did not condemn the control order regime. This conclusion clearly troubled former Chief Justice Chaskalson of South Africa:

Control orders may be much worse than they sound. They can require the victim of the order to remain at his or her home for up to 18 hours a day, with constraints upon receiving visitors, attending gatherings, meeting people or going to particular places during the six hours of 'freedom'. We had measures like that in South Africa. We called them house arrest, distinguishing between 12 hours house arrest and 24 hours house arrest. The people affected by such orders found it almost impossible to comply with their terms, resulting in their breaking the orders, which in turn led to their often being prosecuted for doing so.[51]

Meanwhile, there has been gradual erosion of one of the most fundamental safeguards of personal liberty in this country: the limit on the time a person suspected of having committed a terrorist crime may be held in custody without being charged or released. In 1997 the period was four days.[52] In 2000 it was raised to seven days,[53] in 2003 to fourteen days,[54] in 2006 to twenty-eight days.[55] But this was not enough. In late 2005 the government sought to raise the limit to ninety days, although unable to point to a single case where a suspect had been held to the then current limit of fourteen days and released without charge for lack of evidence.[56] This bid was roundly defeated in the House of Commons. Undeterred, the government attempted to increase the period to forty-two days, narrowly succeeding in the House of Commons and abandoning the attempt only after an overwhelming defeat in the House of Lords on 13 October 2008.

Fair hearing guarantees

A fourth similarity between the US and UK responses to terrorism may be found in their erosion of fair hearing guarantees discussed in Chapter 9. In a recent case the Supreme Court of Canada observed, in a unanimous judgment delivered by the Chief Justice: 'Last but not least, a fair hearing requires that the affected person be informed of the case against him or her, and be permitted to respond to that case. This right is well established in immigration law.'[57] The principle was 'that a person whose liberty is in jeopardy must know the case to meet'.[58] On the legislative scheme before it, the court held, 'that principle has not merely been limited; it has been effectively gutted. How can one meet a case one does not know?'[59] The court went on to find that the secrecy required by the scheme denied the named person the opportunity to know the case put against him or her, and hence to challenge the government's case.[60]

In this country, the right of those in jeopardy to know the case against them so that they can answer it has not perhaps been 'effectively gutted'. But it has, as discussed in Chapter 9, been severely restricted in cases where the authorities are unwilling to disclose sensitive security information to those in jeopardy and their lawyers. This is not a situation which proponents of the rule of law can view without unease.

In the United States the starting point is somewhat different. Immigration officials under a series of administrations have asserted the right to rely on undisclosed evidence to detain and deport foreign nationals, contending that non-citizens do not enjoy the same constitutional protection as citizens. This policy had been rejected in a number of courts before 2001, but 9/11 somewhat reversed the tide of judicial opinion and decisions were then given upholding the government's claim to withhold evidence against non-citizens in immigration proceedings. Meanwhile, the PATRIOT Act authorized the government to use classified information, presented behind closed doors, to support the freezing of assets of allegedly terrorist organizations and Muslim charities; it exercised the power also against US citizens accused of supporting proscribed groups. This, Professor Cole has argued, is part of a repeated pattern: extraordinary powers, first exercised only against non-citizens, on the ground that they do not enjoy the constitutional protection extended to citizens, and arousing little protest because applied to non-citizens only, are then extended to citizens also.[61] Any use of evidence which, because secret, cannot be challenged must give grounds for concern: as Judge Damon Keith observed in 2002 when condemning as unconstitutional the US Attorney General's blanket policy of closing to the public all immigration proceedings involving persons of interest to 9/11 investigators, 'Democracies die behind closed doors.'[62]

Torture

A fifth similarity of response may be found in (on the American side) a new approach to torture and (on the British side) at least a certain ambivalence towards it. This is surprising. As noted in Chapter 2, the British Bill of Rights 1689 provides that 'cruel and unusual punishments' shall not be inflicted, a provision copied in the Eighth Amendment to the US Constitution in 1791. Both countries are parties to the Geneva Conventions of 1949, common Article 3 of which prohibits violence to life and person, murder of all kinds, mutilation, cruel treatment, torture, outrages upon personal dignity, and humiliating and degrading treatment. Both countries are parties to the International Covenant on Civil and Political Rights (1966), which in Article 7 provides that no one shall be subjected to torture or to cruel, inhuman or degrading treatment or punishment. Both countries are parties to the UN Convention Against Torture, which requires all states to prevent torture in any territory under their jurisdiction, provides that no exceptional circumstances whatever may be invoked as a justification and requires that acts of torture be treated as criminal.

It might have been supposed that, at the outset of the twenty-first century, nothing could be clearer than the rejection by civilized nations of torture and humiliating and degrading treatment, and the automatic rejection by civilized courts of the evidential fruits of such conduct. Unhappily, as noted above, US officials have, as a deliberate act of policy, rewritten the definition of torture; have inflicted treatment which most of the rest of the world regards as torture and which is now acknowledged by the US Government to be such; and have sought to deny protection against torture or cruel, inhuman and degrading treatment to foreign nationals held abroad, leaving the United States free to do to foreigners abroad what it could not do to Americans at home.[63] When, in *Hamdan v Rumsfeld*,[64] the Supreme Court held that detainees at Guantanamo were protected by Article 3 of the Geneva Conventions, and rejected the military commission system previously established as unfair, Congress legislated in the Military Commissions Act 2006 to decriminalize humiliating and degrading treatment and draw fine, unworkable, distinctions between torture and cruel treatment.[65]

Only an amendment by Senator John McCain prohibited the use by officials of cruel, inhuman and degrading treatment wherever they acted and whatever the nationality of the person being interrogated.[66] When the President signed the Bill he affixed a signing statement signifying that 'the executive branch shall construe [the McCain amendment] in a manner consistent with the constitutional authority of the President to supervise the unitary executive branch and as Commander in Chief and consistent with the constitutional limitations on the judicial power'.[67] An unfriendly journalist translated this as meaning: 'If the President believes torture is warranted to protect the country, he'll violate the law and authorize torture. If the courts try to stop him, he'll ignore them, too.'[68] While evidence obtained by torture was inadmissible under the Military Commissions Act, coerced evidence 'in which the degree of coercion is disputable' might be adduced if the coercion occurred before the date of the McCain amendment, as would have been the case for most of the Guantanamo detainees.[69] Moreover, the Act permits the prosecutor to 'introduce ... evidence ... while protecting from disclosure the ... methods ... by which the United States acquired the evidence if the military judge finds that the ... methods are classified': thus the detainee cannot in that event establish the basis of his objection to the evidence.[70] But these rules only apply under the Act to non-citizens: they are to be tried by military commissions in accordance with the rules of procedure and evidence laid down in the Act, while US citizens are to be tried before the ordinary courts in accordance with US criminal law: all this in a measure commended to Congress by the President as demonstrating the United States' 'commitment to the rule of law'.[71] Happily, the values for which the United States has proudly stood throughout most of its history, since the days when General Washington, during the War of Independence, forbade the torture of British prisoners of war despite the use of torture by the British on American prisoners, have been robustly reasserted by the incoming administration of President Obama.

In addition to the international instruments mentioned above, the UK is also party to the European Convention, Article 3 of which (as noted in Chapter 7) confers an absolute right not to be tortured or subjected to inhuman or degrading treatment. This is an article from which there may be no opt-out, even in an emergency. In a case brought by the Republic of Ireland against the UK in 1978,[72] the European Court had found methods of interrogation used by the UK to be not torture (as the European Commission on Human Rights had held) but inhuman and degrading treatment. But later, as noted in Chapter 7, the Court indicated that standards change and the methods of interrogation might now be regarded as torture.[73] Perhaps chastened by this experience and mindful of the possibility of complaint under the Convention, perhaps on grounds of moral principle, the UK does not appear to have responded to the threat of terrorism since 2001 by resorting to the use of torture and ill-treatment as an instrument of policy. Whether British officials were complicit in the use of torture by others, by encouragement, acquiescence or turning a blind eye, has yet to be investigated and decided. But it cannot be said that the UK has shown that implacable hostility to torture and its fruits which might have been expected of the state whose courts led the world in rejecting them both. In a sequel to the *Belmarsh* case, already mentioned, the Government argued that evidence obtained by torture abroad without the complicity of the British authorities could be considered by the Special Immigration Appeals Commission, a contention which the House of Lords unanimously and strongly rejected.[74]

Reference has been made above to the European Court's decision in *Chahal*, forbidding the deportation of a foreign national, even if he is a security risk, to a country where he stands a real risk of being tortured. That the decision is a very unwelcome impediment to government action cannot be doubted. Dr John Reid (then Home Secretary) described the judgment as 'outrageously disproportionate',[75] and has suggested that those in the House of Commons who defended the decision 'just don't get it'. So the UK has done its best to persuade the European Court to change its mind. To that end it intervened in one case in which an applicant complained of a Dutch decision to deport him to a country where he feared he would be tortured.[76] The UK also intervened in a case in which a Tunisian resident in Italy was threatened with return to Tunisia, where he faced a risk of torture.[77] But the Court strongly reaffirmed its approach in *Chahal*: '[S]tates face immense difficulties in modern times in protecting their communities from terrorist violence. It [the Court] cannot therefore underestimate the scale of the danger of terrorism today and the threat it presents to the community. That must not, however, call into question the absolute nature of Article 3.'[78]

As an alternative means of escaping the *Chahal* prohibition, the UK government has concluded agreements with some proposed destination states in the Middle East and North Africa, including Jordan, Lebanon and Libya, that deportees will not be ill-treated if returned.[79] An agreement with Jordan has been accepted by the British courts as affording the deportee adequate protection, and deportations to Algeria have been permitted on the strength of formal assurances, despite the absence of an agreement.[80] But deportation to Libya was denied, despite the existence of an agreement. This is difficult territory. States which routinely torture detainees rarely admit to doing so, and the UN Committee against Torture was critical of Sweden when it returned an asylum-seeker to Egypt on the basis of 'assurances from the Egyptian authorities with respect to future treatment', when Sweden knew, or should have known, that 'Egypt resorted to consistent and widespread use of torture against detainees, and that the risk of such treatment was particularly high in the case of detainees held for political and security reasons'.[81]

Surveillance

A sixth similarity between the response of the United States and the UK to 9/11 has been heightened surveillance by governmental authorities of members of the public. In the United States, steps were initially taken which were unlawful, but they were judicially condemned, aroused strong public protest when they became known, were limited in extent and were brought to an end. In the UK the danger is that the country may (as the Information Commissioner put it, reported by the BBC News on 2 November 2006) sleepwalk into a surveillance society. The steps taken have not been unlawful, and public protest has been muted. But within a short period of time we have become the most closely monitored people in the free world.

In the United States, the Foreign Intelligence Surveillance Act 1978 permitted the government to intercept the telephone conversations and e-mails, without showing probable grounds for suspicion, of persons believed to be associated with a foreign power. But such wire-tapping could lawfully take place only if authorized by a warrant issued by a judge before or immediately after the wire-tap took place. There was thus, as in Britain (although the procedures are different), a legal framework, laid down in statute, governing interception of communications. But in the aftermath of 9/11 the Bush administration, in pursuance of its preventive paradigm, departed from this rule. By a secret order, the President authorized the National Security Agency to intercept communications without any judicial warrant, thus bypassing Congress and authorizing violations of federal criminal law.[82] It took some time for the order to become public but when it did it was challenged, and in August 2006 a federal judge sitting in Michigan (Judge Anna Diggs Taylor) ruled that it violated the terms of the Act. As the Supreme Court had done, she rejected the government's argument that the President's action was within his authority as Commander-in-Chief, writing that 'there are no hereditary Kings in America'.[83] (Her decision was overruled by the US Court of Appeals a year later, and the Supreme Court declined to hear an appeal.) Referring to a similar situation, former President Nixon had asserted, in the course of an interview with David Frost, that 'when the President does it, that means it is not illegal',[84] but this approach did not prevail. Rejected by the court, and opposed by the court responsible for authorizing wire-taps,[85] President Bush's secret order also provoked widespread opposition among the public, and in January 2007 he announced the abandonment of his warrantless wire-tapping programme.[86]

In the UK, statutory provision was made in 1985 for the interception of communications where one of a number of specified grounds was shown.[87] It was necessary for a warrant to be obtained in advance signed by a secretary of state; the issue of warrants was retrospectively scrutinized by a judge, whether serving or retired; mistakes were relatively few; and the number of interceptions was relatively modest. But since enactment of the Regulation of Investigatory Powers Act 2000, the situation has changed. More than 650 public bodies are empowered to obtain communications data, including all 474 local authorities in the country. They may exercise this power for the purpose of preventing and detecting those suspected of crime, who may include rogue traders, fly-tippers and fraudsters. Similar powers are exercisable by, among others, 52 police forces and 110 other public authorities who between them, in the period 1 April–31 December 2006, generated 253,577 requests for communications data.[88] All journeys undertaken on motorways and through city centres are recorded by the network of automatic number-plate-recognition cameras.[89] The UK has been said to have more than 4 million CCTV cameras, and the largest DNA database in the world, said to have more than 4.25 million entries, covering one in every fourteen inhabitants[90] (although some entries may, it seems, be scrapped). According to a dossier recently compiled by a minister, there are more than 1,000 laws and regulations which permit officials to force entry into homes, cars and business premises.[91] Of 753 statutory provisions and 290 regulations giving such authority, nearly half (430) have been introduced since 1997. According to a survey by Privacy International, the UK is now the most closely watched country in Europe, prompting a commentator to note that 'Germany, a country with a unique 20th century double experience – Nazi and Stasi – of unfreedom, is now, according to Privacy International, the least watched.'[92]

The greatly increased level of surveillance in Britain is, of course, made possible by the notable technological advances witnessed in recent years. But it seems clear that the urge to know and record more and more about members of the public has been strengthened by experience of 9/11 and the bombings of July 2005. The main reaction of the public to this steady encroachment by the state into what had been regarded as the private domain of the citizen has been one of apathy, save in relation to the proposal for a universal identity card carrying extensive personal biometric data. This apathy may be because the end (preventing terrorist violence, catching criminals) is thought to justify the means; it may be because most people are unaware of what is happening; or it may be because, surveillance being covert, no one knows that they are being watched, their movements recorded, their communications intercepted or monitored.

One eloquent and persistent critic of our descent into a surveillance society (Henry Porter, writing in the *Observer*) has pointed to the history outlined above as demonstrating the failure of the Human Rights Act.[93] That is a fair criticism, up to a point. But breaches of the Act can be found by the courts only if complaints are made which come

THE RULE OF LAW

before the courts for adjudication. Such complaints could have been made under Article 8 of the European Convention, as briefly described in Chapter 7. But there have been very few such complaints, and one can only speculate how they would have been resolved if made. From a libertarian viewpoint the outcome in Britain is much less desirable than that in the United States: but, as matters stand, the British government (unlike the American) can claim to have complied with the rule of law in the field of public surveillance.

The war in Iraq

The seventh and last similarity between the US and UK responses to 9/11 may be found, I suggest, in their joint invasion of Iraq, discussed in Chapter 10. But this involves a paradox. The invasion was a response in the sense that, but for 9/11, there would have been no invasion. That seems clear. But if one asks what Iraq, or Saddam Hussein, had to do with 9/11 the answer is, and has always appeared to be: nothing. No reasonable person could do other than condemn the brutal and tyrannical regime of Saddam Hussein, but one crime which cannot be laid at his door is responsibility for 9/11. I have given in Chapter 10 my reasons for concluding that the invasion of Iraq violated the rule of law.

Conclusion

The advent of serious terrorist violence, carried out by those willing to die in the cause of killing others, tests adherence to the rule of law to the utmost: for states, as is their duty, strain to protect their people against the consequences of such violence, and the strong temptation exists to cross the boundary which separates the lawful from the unlawful.

Is there, in this exigency any principle to which we can cling? Yes. Such a principle was articulated by the Council of Europe in 2002:

The temptation for governments and parliaments in countries suffering from terrorist action is to fight fire with fire, setting aside the legal safeguards that exist in a democratic state. But let us be clear about this: while the State has the right to employ to the full its arsenal of legal weapons to repress and prevent terrorist activities, it may not use indiscriminate measures which would only undermine the fundamental values they seek to protect. For a State to react in such a way would be to fall into the trap set by terrorism for democracy and the rule of law.[94]

A similar principle was recognized by the International Commission of Jurists in their Berlin Declaration of 28 August 2004:

In adopting measures aimed at suppressing acts of terrorism, states must adhere strictly to the rule of law, including the core principles of criminal and international law and the specific standards and obligations of international human rights law, refugee law and, where applicable, humanitarian law. These principles, standards and obligations define the boundaries of permissible and legitimate state action against terrorism. The odious nature of terrorist acts cannot serve as a basis or pretext for states to disregard their international obligations, in particular in the protection of fundamental human rights.[95]

But perhaps the last word should lie with a great Catholic thinker, Christopher Dawson, who wrote in 1943, when Britain and the United States were pitted against the great evil of Nazism, 'As soon as men decide that all means are permitted to fight an evil then their good becomes indistinguishable from the evil that they set out to destroy.'[96] There may, of course, be those who would think this a 'dangerous misjudgment'.

12

The Rule of Law and the Sovereignty of Parliament

If asked to identify the predominant characteristics of our constitutional settlement in the United Kingdom today, most of us would, I think, point to, or at any rate include in any list, our commitment to the rule of law and our recognition of the Queen in Parliament as the supreme law-making authority in the country. We would regard our commitment to the rule of law as one which, allowing for some flexibility and variation, we broadly share with other liberal democracies around the world. Our acceptance of parliamentary sovereignty, by contrast, distinguishes us from all other members of the European Union, the United States, almost all the former Dominions and those former colonies to which this country granted independent constitutions. In all these countries the constitution, interpreted by the courts, has been the supreme law of the land, with the result that legislation inconsistent with the constitution, even if duly enacted, may be held to be unconstitutional and so invalid. While preserving our inalienable right to be discontented with the government of the day, and probably with the opposition also, I do not think there has been any groundswell of dissatisfaction with our acceptance of parliamentary sovereignty, even if we do not quite share the complacency of Anthony Trollope's view of the political scene in 1859:

At home in England, Crown, Lords and Commons really seem to do very well. Some may think that the system wants a little shove this way, some the other. Reform may, or may not be, more or less needed. But on the whole we are governed honestly, liberally and successfully, with at least a greater share of honesty, liberality, and success than has fallen to the lot of most other people. Each of the three estates enjoys the respect of the people at large, and a seat, either among the Lords or the Commons, is an object of high ambition. The system may therefore be said to be successful.[1]

But respected and authoritative voices now question whether parliamentary sovereignty can coexist with the rule of law. In his recent, very distinguished, Hamlyn Lectures (*The Sovereignty of Law: The European Way*), Professor Sir Francis Jacobs observes:

Legally, it is difficult, if not impossible, to identify today a State in which a 'sovereign' legislature is not subject to legal limitations on the exercise of its powers. Moreover, sovereignty is incompatible, both internationally and internally, with another concept which also has a lengthy history, but which today is widely regarded as a paramount value: the rule of law.[2]

The rule of law, he continued, 'cannot coexist with traditional conceptions of sovereignty'.[3] In similar vein, Professor Vernon Bogdanor, Professor of Government at Oxford, recently thought it 'clear that there is a conflict between these two constitutional principles, the sovereignty of Parliament and the rule of law', a conflict which if not resolved could generate a constitutional crisis.[4] Reflecting this view, some distinguished academic authors,[5] and also some judges in extrajudicial utterances[6] and obiter observations,[7] have suggested that Parliament is not, or is no longer, supreme and that in some circumstances the judges might, without the authority of Parliament, hold a statute to be invalid and of no effect because contrary to a higher, fundamental, law or to the rule of law itself. If this is the correct view, the rule of law and parliamentary sovereignty are not, as one might have hoped, a happily married couple but are actual or potential antagonists. This makes it necessary to supplement this book's discussion of the rule of law by a closer look at parliamentary sovereignty. It cannot be treated as a concept which, in the time-honoured formula used of lecturers and after-dinner speakers, is so well known as to call for no introduction.

Professor Bogdanor has pointed out that the essence of parliamentary sovereignty can be expressed in eight words: 'What the Queen in Parliament enacts is law.'[8] In a memorable aphorism which Professor Dicey borrowed from an eighteenth-century writer[9] and made famous: 'It is a fundamental principle with English lawyers, that Parliament can do everything but make a woman a man, and a man a woman.'[10] Thus there was and could be no fundamental or constitutional law which Parliament could not change by the ordinary process of legislation. This does not of course mean that Parliament is omnipotent. Even the most paranoid legislator could not suppose that the due enactment of a statute at Westminster could effectively proscribe smoking on the streets of New York or the consumption of vodka in Russia. What the principle means is that Parliament has, in the United Kingdom, no legislative superior. The courts have no inherent powers to invalidate, strike down, supersede or disregard the provisions of an unambiguous statute duly enacted by the Queen in Parliament, and, indeed, an extremely limited power to enquire whether a statute has been duly enacted.[11] So to express the principle is to expose the conflict or incompatibility to which I have already referred. For if Parliament may, under our constitution, enact any legislation it chooses, and no court has any power to annul or modify such enactment, it necessarily follows that Parliament can legislate so as to abrogate or infringe any human right, no matter how fundamental it may be thought to be, or any obligation binding on the United Kingdom in international law. The courts have faced up to this problem. In the words of one notable judicial authority on constitutional issues:

If the terms of the legislation are clear and unambiguous, they must be given effect to, whether or not they carry out Her Majesty's treaty obligations, for the sovereign power of the Queen in Parliament extends to breaking treaties [authority cited], and any remedy for such a breach of an international obligation lies in a forum other than Her Majesty's own courts.[12]

The same rule must apply to the infringement of fundamental human rights. Such an approach is consistent with what, in Chapter 7, I called the 'thin' definition of the rule of law, less so with the 'thick' definition.

Thus, critics of parliamentary sovereignty have no difficulty conceiving of flagrantly unjust and objectionable statutes: to deprive Jews of their nationality, to prohibit Christians from marrying non-Christians, to dissolve marriages between blacks and whites, to confiscate the property of red-haired women, to require all blue-eyed babies to be killed, to deprive large sections of the population of the right to vote, to authorize officials to inflict punishment for whatever reason they might choose.[13] No one thinks it at all likely that Parliament would enact legislation of this character, or that the public would accept it if it did, but it is possible to conceive of less extreme and less improbable statutes which would nonetheless infringe fundamental rights, and the mere possibility that Parliament might act in such a way gives rise to the argument that parliamentary sovereignty cannot, or cannot any longer, be fully respected.

Those who seek to undermine the principle of parliamentary sovereignty draw sustenance from the observation of Sir Edward Coke in *Dr Bonham's Case* in 1610 that a statute contrary to common right and reason would be void.[14] But it is not entirely clear what Coke meant;[15] it appears that this observation may have been added after judgment had been given;[16] it did not represent his later view;[17] it was relied on as one of the reasons for his dismissal as Chief Justice of the King's Bench;[18] and it was not a view which commanded general acceptance even at the time.[19] As Professor Jeffrey Goldsworthy has shown in his magisterial book on *The Sovereignty of Parliament*, on which I have drawn heavily and to which I am much indebted, there is no recorded case in which the courts, without the authority of Parliament, have invalidated or struck down a statute. This point is not to be discounted by pointing out, although this is true, that the question has never arisen for decision, since that is itself significant. As Goldsworthy demonstrates, to my mind wholly convincingly, the principle of parliamentary sovereignty has been endorsed without reservation by the greatest authorities on our constitutional, legal and cultural history. I need only mention Lord Burghley, Sir Robert Cecil, Sir Matthew Hale, Francis Bacon, John Selden, John Locke, the Marquess of Halifax, Blackstone, Adam Smith, Samuel Johnson, Lord Hardwicke, Montesquieu, Thomas Paine, Maitland, Holdsworth, Dicey.[20] As was stated by the Court of Queen's Bench in 1872: 'There is no judicial body in the country by which the validity of an act of parliament could be questioned. An act of the legislature is superior in authority to any court of law ... and no court could pronounce a judgment as to the validity of an act of parliament.'[21] John James Park, one of the first professors of law at King's College, London, declared with similar clarity in 1832 that the British Constitution had no fundamental laws that could not be changed in the same way as ordinary laws.[22] He quoted an American author who had written:

This is admitted by English jurists to be the case in respect to their own constitution, which, in all its vital parts, may be changed by an act of parliament; that is, the king, lords, and commons may, if they think proper, abrogate and repeal any existing laws, and pass any new laws in direct opposition to that which the people contemplate and revere as their ancient constitution. No such laws can be ... declared void by the courts of justice as unconstitutional.[23]

A more favoured argument advanced by those seeking to undermine the principle of parliamentary sovereignty is that Parliament's sovereignty was but is no longer absolute. Three examples are usually given to support this contention: the European Communities Act 1972, the Human Rights Act 1998 and the three 1998 Acts devolving a measure of power to Scotland, Wales and Northern Ireland. None of these examples, I suggest, supports the proposition contended for: all involve a curtailment of the Westminster Parliament's power to legislate, but that curtailment takes effect by express authority of the Westminster Parliament, which, at least theoretically, it retains the power to revoke.

Sections 2 and 3 of the European Communities Act 1972, enacted upon the UK becoming a member, provided in effect that the law of the Communities should have effect in this country. Before this date the European Court of Justice had already decided that the provisions of the Treaty of Rome had direct effect in member states and that Community law enjoyed primacy over any inconsistent national law of a member state.[24] It necessarily followed that if a national parliament were to legislate inconsistently with a relevant provision of Community law, as the UK Parliament did when it enacted the Merchant Shipping Act 1988 and the Employment Protection (Consolidation) Act 1978, the statute would be wholly or in part invalid, as was in due course held in two leading cases.[25] This is the best example from the critics' point of view, since the process does involve the invalidation of statutes by the courts. But the courts act in that way only because Parliament, exercising its legislative authority, has told them to. If Parliament, exercising the same authority, told them not to do so, they would obey that injunction also.

The supposed exception based on the Human Rights Act is even weaker. As widely appreciated (although not, surprisingly, by Tony Blair, the Prime Minister whose government promoted the Act), it was carefully drafted so as to preclude the invalidation by the courts of domestic legislation inconsistent with the articles of the European Convention given domestic effect by the Act. It provided instead for the higher courts to make declarations of incompatibility which ministers might take steps to rectify, but were not obliged under the Act so to do.[26] In the White Paper introducing the Human Rights Bill, to which Mr Blair contributed the preface, the scheme of the legislation was made very plain:

The Government has reached the conclusion that courts should not have the power to set aside primary legislation, past or future, on the ground of incompatibility with the Convention. This conclusion arises from the importance which the Government attaches to Parliamentary sovereignty. In this context, Parliamentary sovereignty means that Parliament is competent to make any law on any matter of its choosing and no court may question the validity of any Act that it passes ... To make provision in the Bill for the courts to set aside Acts of Parliament would confer on the judiciary a general power over the decisions of Parliament which under our present constitutional arrangements they do not possess, and would be likely on occasions to draw the judiciary into serious conflict with Parliament. There is no evidence to suggest that they desire this power, nor that the public wish them to have it ... [27]

Thus, in applying the Human Rights Act the courts have what has been called 'a very specific, wholly democratic, mandate',[28] but it is a mandate from Parliament and not one which overrides the sovereign legislative authority of the Queen in Parliament.

The devolution legislation affecting Scotland, Wales and Northern Ireland was of course prompted by the view that distinctive national communities within the United Kingdom should have increased responsibility for managing their own affairs. So Parliament enacted that certain functions which it and some central government departments had previously carried out should be devolved to the local administrations. But this involved no irrevocable surrender of parliamentary sovereignty, as is made clear by section 28(7) of the Scotland

Act: 'This section does not affect the power of the Parliament of the United Kingdom to make laws for Scotland.' The Northern Irish Act contains a similar provision.[29]

It has been suggested, with some judicial support,[30] that the principle of parliamentary sovereignty did not apply in Scotland before the Act of Union in 1707 and that the Union with Scotland Act 1706 cannot itself be amended or abrogated since it gave effect to the Treaty of Union, in which certain provisions were agreed to be, and were described in the Act as, 'unalterable'. The merits of this argument are far from clear.[31] It is hard to see how the pre-1707 Scottish Parliament could have done anything more fundamental than abolish itself (which is what it did), and it is hard to accept that the Westminster Parliament could not modify the Act of Union if there were a clear majority in favour of doing so. But if, which I doubt, there is an exception here to the principle of parliamentary sovereignty, it is a very limited exception born of the peculiar circumstances pertaining to the union with Scotland and throws no doubt on the general applicability of the principle.

Much interest has been generated by observations of my greatly respected former colleague Lord Steyn in the case brought to challenge the validity of the Hunting Act 2004.[32] His observations did not bear on an issue which was argued or had to be decided in the case, and therefore have no authority as precedent, but they are germane to the question I am considering. He said:

The classic account given by Dicey of the doctrine of the supremacy of Parliament, pure and absolute as it was, can now be seen to be out of place in the modern United Kingdom. Nevertheless, the supremacy of Parliament is still the *general* principle of our constitution. It is a construct of the common law. The judges created this principle. If that is so, it is not unthinkable that circumstances could arise where the courts may have to qualify a principle established on a different hypothesis of constitutionalism. In exceptional circumstances involving an attempt to abolish judicial review or the ordinary role of the courts, the Appellate Committee of the House of Lords or a new Supreme Court may have to consider whether this is [a] constitutional fundamental which even a sovereign Parliament acting at the behest of a complaisant House of Commons cannot abolish.[33]

Lord Hope of Craighead similarly described the principle of parliamentary sovereignty as having been 'created by the common law',[34] that is, by the judges. Baroness Hale of Richmond added: 'The courts will treat with particular suspicion (and might even reject) any attempt to subvert the rule of law by removing governmental action affecting the rights of the individual from all judicial scrutiny.'[35] Welcomed in some quarters, these observations have also been described by one acerbic academic commentator as 'unargued and unsound', 'historically false' and 'jurisprudentially absurd'.[36] No authority was cited to support them, and no detailed reasons were given.

I cannot for my part accept that my colleagues' observations are correct. It is true of course that the principle of parliamentary sovereignty cannot without circularity be ascribed to statute, and the historical record in any event reveals no such statute. But it does not follow that the principle must be a creature of the judge-made common law which the judges can alter: if it were, the rule could be altered by statute, since the prime characteristic of any common law rule is that it yields to a contrary provision of statute. To my mind, it has been convincingly shown[37] that the principle of parliamentary sovereignty has been recognized as fundamental in this country not because the judges invented it but because it has for centuries been accepted as such by judges and others officially concerned in the operation of our constitutional system. The judges did not by themselves establish the principle and they cannot, by themselves, change it.

This is not a conclusion which, thus far, I regret, for the reason very well expressed by Professor Goldsworthy:

What is at stake is the location of ultimate decision-making authority – the right to the 'final word' – in a legal system. If the judges were to repudiate the doctrine of parliamentary sovereignty, by refusing to allow Parliament to infringe unwritten rights, they would be claiming that ultimate authority for themselves. In settling disagreements about what fundamental rights people have, and whether legislation is consistent with them, the judges' word rather than Parliament's would be final. Since virtually all significant moral and political controversies in contemporary Western societies involve disagreements about rights, this would amount to a massive transfer of political power from parliaments to judges. Moreover, it would be a transfer of power initiated by the judges, to protect rights chosen by them, rather than one brought about democratically by parliamentary enactment or popular referendum. It is no wonder that the elected branches of government regard that prospect with apprehension.[38]

I agree. The British people have not repelled the extraneous power of the papacy in spiritual matters and the pretensions of royal power in temporal in order to subject themselves to the unchallengeable rulings of unelected judges. A constitution should reflect the will of a clear majority of the people, and a constitutional change of the kind here contemplated should be made in accordance with that will or not at all. As it was put by a Member of Parliament in 1621: 'the judges are judges of the law, not of the Parliament. God forbid the state of the kingdom should ever come under the sentence of a judge.'[39]

Thus, for those who have followed me this far, we reach these conclusions. We live in a society dedicated to the rule of law; in which Parliament has power, subject to limited, self-imposed restraints, to legislate as it wishes; in which Parliament may therefore legislate in a way which infringes the rule of law; and in which the judges, consistently with their constitutional duty to administer justice according to the laws and usages of the realm, cannot fail to give effect to such legislation if it is clearly and unambiguously expressed. Is there, then, a vice at the heart of our constitutional system? Some would answer that there is not, since although Parliament has the theoretical power to legislate in a way that infringes the rule of law and fundamental rights it can in practice be relied on not to do so. No doubt the prospect of legislation discriminating against blue-eyed babies or red-haired women can be effectively discounted. But it is not at all hard to envisage legislation infringing the rule of law in less obvious ways (as, for example, by legislating to preclude any legal challenge to decisions of a statutory tribunal, as was proposed in clause 11 of the Asylum and Immigration (Treatment of Claimants etc.) Bill 2004, later withdrawn[40]) and a constitution should, ideally, give protection against minor aberrations as well as those which are gross. Under the constitutional settlement bequeathed to us by the Glorious Revolution, a substantial measure of protection was given by the requirement that

Crown, Lords and Commons, each of them powerful independent players, should assent to legislation before it became law. As a Victorian Lord Chief Justice put it in 1846: 'The constitution has lodged the sacred deposit of sovereign authority in a chest locked by three different keys, confided to the custody of three different trustees.'[41] Referring to these three different trustees, the same author continued with what now seems extraordinary prescience: 'One of them is now at length, after ages of struggle, effectually prevented from acting alone; but another of the two is said to enjoy the privilege of striking off the two other locks, when, for any purpose of its own, it wishes to lay hands on the treasure.'

Today, as we know, the legislative role of the Crown has been reduced to mere formality, and under the Parliament Acts 1911 and 1949 the power of the Lords is one of relatively brief delay and not denial. It was originally envisaged that the 1911 Act should be used to effect only major constitutional changes, and it was so used to enact the Government of Ireland Act 1914, the Welsh Church Act 1914 and the Parliament Act 1949 itself. But the 1949 Act has been used in recent years to achieve objects of more minor or no constitutional import (the War Crimes Act 1991, the European Parliamentary Elections Act 1999, the Sexual Offences (Amendment) Act 2000 and the Hunting Act 2004). This is the 'elective dictatorship' to which Lord Hailsham, out of office at the time, famously referred, as mentioned in Chapter 2. Thus our constitutional settlement has become unbalanced, and the power to restrain legislation favoured by a clear majority of the Commons has become much weakened, even if, exceptionally, such legislation were to infringe the rule of law as I have defined it. This calls for consideration as a serious problem. It is not a problem which will go away if we ignore it, but it may perhaps give rise, as Professor Bogdanor fears, to wholly undesirable conflict between Parliament and the judges. It could also lead to undesirable constitutional uncertainty. The last ten or twelve years have seen a degree of constitutional change not experienced for centuries. Important questions (such as the composition and role of the House of Lords and the system used to elect members of the House of Commons) remain unresolved. One may hope that the sovereignty of Parliament and its relationship with the rule of law may be seen as a matter worthy of consideration if, as I suggest, there are some rules which no government should be free to violate without legal restraint. To substitute the sovereignty of a codified and entrenched Constitution for the sovereignty of Parliament is, however, a major constitutional change. It is one which should be made only if the British people, properly informed, choose to make it.[42]

Epilogue

In September 2005 the Council of the International Bar Association passed a resolution in which it said:

The Rule of Law is the foundation of a civilised society. It establishes a transparent process accessible and equal to all. It ensures adherence to principles that both liberate and protect. The IBA calls upon all countries to respect these fundamental principles. It also calls upon its members to speak out in support of the Rule of Law within their respective communities.

While the resolution attempted no definition, it listed certain components of the rule of law, among them an independent, impartial judiciary, the presumption of innocence and the right to a fair and public trial without undue delay. It described as 'unacceptable' arbitrary arrests, secret trials, indefinite detention without trial, cruel or degrading treatment or punishment and intimidation or corruption in the electoral process.

Following this resolution the Association convened four symposia devoted to the rule of law in 2006–7: in Chicago, Moscow, Singapore and Buenos Aires. The tangible outcome was a book: *The Rule of Law: Perspectives from Around the Globe*,[1] edited by Francis Neate, a distinguished English solicitor who was President of the Association in 2005 and 2006, and inspired this initiative.

There is much common ground in the approach of the different speakers. Thus Anne Ramberg, chief executive of the Swedish Bar Association, said:

The Rule of Law requires many things. It requires adequate legislation duly adopted. There is a requirement as to form. But there is also a qualitative threshold. The law must properly incorporate societal values including the demands of human rights and international humanitarian law. But not even that is enough. The Rule of Law also requires a proper administration of justice. This in turn mandates a reliable and qualitative court system with well educated and honest judges, prosecutors and advocates.[2]

Part of the address of V. D. Zorkin, President of the Constitutional Court of the Russian Federation, was quoted in Chapter 7.

In the view of Genry Reznik, President of the Moscow City Chamber of Advocates, 'The Rule of Law is especially important as an influence on economic development in developing and emerging markets'. Sir Gerard Brennan, formerly Chief Justice of Australia, listed a number of what he called 'characteristic features of the Rule of Law': public promulgation of laws made by the democratic process; public administration of the law; impartial application of the law; observance of natural justice; the doing of justice according to law; the universal application of the law.[3]

Mr S. Jayakumar, Deputy Prime Minister, Co-ordinating Minister for National Security and Minister for Law of Singapore, was clear in his view:

The Rule of Law concept, in essence, embodies a number of important inter-related ideas. First, there should be clear limits to the power of the state. A government exercises its authority through publicly disclosed laws that are adopted and enforced by an independent judiciary in accordance with established and accepted procedures. Secondly, no one is above the law; there is equality before the law. Thirdly, there must be protection of the rights of the individual.

In modern society, the value of the Rule of Law is that it is essential for good governance. Governments must govern in accordance with established laws and conventions and not in an arbitrary manner. The law must set out legitimate expectations about what is acceptable behaviour and conduct of both the governed and the government. This is important: the law must apply equally to the government and individual citizens.[4]

Judge Hisashi Owada, a judge of the International Court of Justice, like Sir Gerard Brennan listed key components of the rule of law:

restraint on state autonomy in inter-state relations; the supremacy of the law; equality before the law; separation of powers; the independence of the judiciary; the international rule of law in relation to the individual.[5]

Sternford Moyo, former president of the Law Society of Zimbabwe, drew attention to a declaration on the rule of law made by the International Commission of Jurists at Athens in 1955. It provided that:

1. the State is subject to the law;
2. governments should respect the rights of individuals under the Rule of Law and provide effective means for their enforcement;
3. judges should be guided by the Rule of Law, protect and enforce it without fear or favour and resist any encroachment by governments or political parties in their independence as judges;
4. lawyers of the world should preserve the independence of their profession, assert the rights of an individual under the Rule of Law and insist that every accused is accorded a fair trial.[6]

There is nothing here at which, half a century later, one would wish to cavil. He went on, as others had done, to list the characteristics of a society in which the rule of law is observed: a general clarity of the law; the existence of a climate of legality; the existence of an adequate and justiciable bill of rights; the existence of an independent judiciary; the existence of an independent legal profession.[7]

These are fine aspirations. But aspiration without action is sterile. It is deeds that matter. We are enjoined to be 'doers of the word, and not hearers only'.[8] And it is on observance of the rule of law that the quality of government depends.

In the Hall of the Nine in the Palazzo Pubblico in Siena is Ambrogio Lorenzetti's depiction of the *Allegory of Good Government*. Justice, as always, is personified as a woman, gesturing towards the scales of justice, held by the personification of Wisdom. At her feet is Virtue, also a woman. A judge sits in the centre, surrounded by figures including Peace. The *Allegory* is flanked by two other paintings, illustrating the *Effects of Good Government* and the *Effects of Bad Government*. In the first, well-to-do merchants ply their trade, the populace dance in the streets and in the countryside well-tended fields yield a plentiful harvest. The second (badly damaged) is a scene of violence, disease and decay. What makes the difference between Good and Bad Government?

I would answer, no doubt predictably: the rule of law. The concept of the rule of law is not fixed for all time. Some countries do not subscribe to it fully, and some subscribe only in name, if that. Even those who do subscribe to it find it difficult to apply all its precepts quite all the time. But in a world divided by differences of nationality, race, colour, religion and wealth it is one of the greatest unifying factors, perhaps the greatest, the nearest we are likely to approach to a universal secular religion. It remains an ideal, but an ideal worth striving for, in the interests of good government and peace, at home and in the world at large.

Notes

CHAPTER 1. THE IMPORTANCE
OF THE RULE OF LAW

1. Brian Z. Tamanaha, *On the Rule of Law* (Cambridge University Press, 2004), pp. 8–9.

2. *Aristotle's Politics and Athenian Constitution*, ed. and trans. John Warrington (J. M. Dent, 1959), book III, s. 1287, p. 97.

3. J. W. F. Allison, *The English Historical Constitution* (Cambridge University Press, 2007), p. 130, n. 11, p. 154, p. 157, n. 2.

4. 'The Mersey Docks and Harbour Board' Trustees: *William Gibbs and Others* (1866) LR 1 HL 93, 110.

5. Allison, *English Historical Constitution*, p. 130, n. 11, referring to W. E. Hearn, *The Government of England: Its Structure and Development* (Longmans, Green, 1867), chap. 3, para. 7.

6. A. V. Dicey, *An Introduction to the Study of the Law of the Constitution* (1885; 9th edn., Macmillan, 1945), p. 188.

7. Ibid., p. 193.

8. Lord Denning, the Master of the Rolls, quoted this in *Gouriet v Union of Post Office Workers* [1977] QB 729, 762, when he thought the Attorney General of the day had overstepped the mark – wrongly, as the House of Lords was later to hold: [1978] AC 435. It seems he was quoting from Dr Fuller's *Gnomologia: Adagies and Proverbs* (1733), in which the sentence quoted was numbered 943.

9. Dicey, *Introduction*, p. 195.

10. As I suggested in 'Dicey Revisited' [2002] PL 39, 46–8.

11. They were strongly reflected in the work which Lord Hewart, as Lord Chief Justice, wrote in 1929: *The New Despotism* (Ernest Benn). Hewart strongly believed that unaccountable power was being exercised by ministers and bureaucrats, in a manner alien to Dicey's thinking.

12. Bingham, 'Dicey Revisited', p. 51.

13. Joseph Raz, 'The Rule of Law and its Virtue', in Raz, *The Authority of Law: Essays on Law and Morality* (Oxford University Press, 1979), p. 210.

14. John Finnis, *Natural Law and Natural Rights* (Oxford University Press, 1980), p. 270.

15. Judith Shklar, 'Political Theory and the Rule of Law', in A. Hutchinson and P. Monahan (eds.), *The Rule of Law: Ideal or Ideology* (Carswell, Toronto, 1987), p. 1.

16. Thomas Carothers, 'Promoting the Rule of Law Abroad', Carnegie Endowment for International Peace, Rule of Law Series, No. 34 (January 2003), p. 3.

17. 531 US 98 (2000).

18. Jeremy Waldron, 'Is the Rule of Law an Essentially Contested Concept (in Florida)?', in R. Bellamy (ed.), *The Rule of Law and Separation of Powers* (Ashgate, 2005), p. 119.

19. Tamanaha, *On the Rule of Law*, p. 3.

20. For recent examples, see *R v Horseferry Road Magistrates' Court, ex p. Bennett* [1994] 1 AC 42, 62, 64, 67, 75, 76, 77; *A v Secretary of State for the Home Department* [2005] 2 AC 68, [2004] UKHL 56, paras. 2, 74.

21. *R v Secretary of State for the Home Department, ex p. Pierson* [1998] AC 539, 591.

22. *R (Alconbury Developments Ltd. and Others) v Secretary of State for the Environment, Transport and the Regions* [2001] UKHL 23, [2003] 2 AC 295, [2001] UKHL 23, para. 73.

23. *R (Corner House Research and another) v Director of the Serious Fraud Office (JUSTICE intervening)* [2008] UKHL 60, [2009] 1 AC 756.

24. John Locke, *Second Treatise of Government*, chap. XVII, s. 202 (1690; Cambridge University Press, 1988), p. 400.

25. Thomas Paine, *Common Sense* (1776; Oxford University Press (World's Classics), 1995), p. 34.

26. Piero Calamandrei, *A Eulogy of Judges* (Princeton University Press, 1942, repr. 1992), chap. XII, p. 95.

CHAPTER 2. SOME HISTORY

1. Sir W. Holdsworth, *A History of English Law*, vol. 2 (4th edn., Methuen/Sweet & Maxwell, 1936), p. 215.

2. J. C. Holt, *Magna Carta and Medieval Government* (Hambledon Press, 1985), p. 196.

3. W. S. McKechnie, *Magna Carta* (2nd edn., James Maclehose, Glasgow, 1914), p. 395.

4. J. C. Holt, *Magna Carta* (Cambridge University Press, 1992), pp. 276–8.

5. McKechnie, *Magna Carta*, pp. 94–5.

6. Holt, *Magna Carta* (1992), p. 295.

7. Ernest Renan, quoted in E. J. Hobsbawm, *Nations and Nationalism Since 1780: Programme, Myth, Reality* (Cambridge University Press, 1990), p. 12.

8. David V. Stivison, 'Magna Carta in American Law', in Stivison (ed.), *Magna Carta in America* (Gateway Press Inc., Baltimore, 1993), p. 103.

9. I base my summary on the helpful account of R. J. Sharpe, *The Law of Habeas Corpus* (2nd edn., Oxford University Press, 1989), pp. 1–8.

10. Holdsworth, *History of English Law*, vol. 9, pp. 104–14.

11. Ibid., p. 104.

12. *Bushell's Case* (1670) Vaughan 135, 136.

13. Some of the relevant history, and a number of the relevant references, are to be found in the opinions of the House of Lords in *A v Secretary of State for the Home Department (No. 2)* [2005] UKHL 71, [2006] 2 AC 221, particularly in paras. 11–12, 64–5, 81, 103–8, 129.

14. D. Jardine, *A Reading on the Use of Torture in the Criminal Law of England Previously to the Commonwealth* (1837), pp. 6, 12.

15. See *A (No. 2)*, above (n. 13), paras. 11, 64, 81.

16. See J. A. Guy, 'The Origins of the Petition of Right Reconsidered', *Historical Journal* (1982), pp. 289–312; M. B. Young, 'The Origins of the Petition of Right Reconsidered Further', *Historical Journal* (1984), pp. 449–52; Mark Kishlansky, 'Tyranny Denied: Charles I, Attorney General Heath, and the "Five Knights" Case', *Historical Journal* (1999), pp. 58–83.

17. *Parliaments and English Politics 1621–1629* (Oxford University Press, 1979), pp. 344, 343.

18. See Robert C. Johnson *et al.* (eds.), *Commons Debates 1628* (Yale Center for Parliamentary History, 1977), vol. 3, p. 98.

19. Ibid., vol. 2, p. 63.

20. Russell, *Parliaments and English Politics*, p. 350.

21. Elizabeth Read Foster, 'Printing the Petition of Right', *Huntington Library Quarterly*, 38/1 (November 1974), pp. 81–2.

22. The text of the Petition is found in many places, conveniently in J. P. Kenyon, *The Stuart Constitution 1603–1688* (2nd edn., Cambridge University Press, 1986), p. 68.

23. *Clarendon* (1668) 6 St Tr 291, 291, 330, 396.

24. G. Burnet, *History of My Own Time* (1897), vol. 1, p. 485.

25. *History of English Law*, vol. 9 (3rd edn., 1944), pp. 117–18 and n. 10.

26. David Lewis Jones, *A Parliamentary History of the Glorious Revolution* (HMSO, 1988), introduction, pp. 24–46.

27. Ibid., p. 49.

28. Holdsworth, *History of English Law*, vol. 6, p. 230.

29. Bill of Rights, I.4, 8.

30. Ibid., I.9.

31. Ibid., I.6.

32. Ibid., I.1.

33. Ibid., I.2.

34. Ibid., XII.

35. Holdsworth, *History of English Law*, vol. 6, p. 240.

36. Bill of Rights, I.10.

37. Ibid.

38. Ibid.

39. Ibid., I.11.

40. Lewis Jones, *Parliamentary History*, p. 29.

41. Ibid., pp. 38–40.

42. Act of Settlement 1701, s. 3.

43. Robert Stevens, 'The Act of Settlement and the Questionable History of Judicial Independence', *Oxford University Commonwealth Law Journal* (2001), p. 259.

44. Holdsworth, *History of English Law*, vol. 6, pp. 234–40.

45. Stevens, 'The Act of Settlement', p. 262.

46. James Boswell, *Life of Johnson*, Oxford Standard Authors, 3rd edn., ed. R. W. Chapman, corrected by J. D. Freeman (Oxford University Press, 1976) pp. 619–20.

47. Richard Henry Lee, in a letter to Samuel Adams, 5 October 1787: see Richard Labinski, *James Madison and the Struggle for the Bill of Rights* (Oxford University Press, 2006), p. 40.

48. In *A Sparrow's Flight* (Collins, 1990), p. 318, Lord Hailsham claimed to have coined this expression, as well as 'unflappable', famously applied to Harold Macmillan in 1958, and the expression 'lunatic fringe'.

49. See, for example, Bernard Bailyn (ed.), *The Debate on the Constitution* (Library of America, 1993), parts 1 and 2.

50. Ibid., part 2, p. 369.

51. See Labinski, *James Madison and the Struggle for the Bill of Rights*.

52. Coleman Phillipson, *The International Law and Custom of Ancient Greece and Rome* (Macmillan, 1911), vol. 2, pp. 166–384.

53. Maurice Keen, *The Laws of War in the Later Middle Ages* (Routledge and Kegan Paul, 1965).

54. See Juliet Barker, *Agincourt* (Abacus, 2006), pp. 169, 223.

55. He was Regius Professor of Civil Law at Oxford when he published his most important work, *De Jure Belli*.

56. *De Jure Belli et Pacis* (1625).

57. See Adam Roberts and Richard Guelff (eds.), *Documents on the Laws of War* (3rd edn., Oxford University Press, 2000), p. 4.

58. Republished by the International Committee of the Red Cross, Geneva, 1986.

59. This Convention was superseded by the first of the four Geneva Conventions of 1949, a greatly expanded version of the ten-article original.

60. See Caroline Moorehead, *Dunant's Dream: War, Switzerland and the History of the Red Cross* (HarperCollins, 1998).

61. See Roberts and Guelff (eds.), *Documents*, pp. 53–7.

62. Ibid., pp. 63–6.

63. Ibid., pp. 67–137.

64. Ibid., pp. 179–94.

65. Ibid., pp. 565–72, 615–21, 667–97.

66. Byelorussia, Czechoslovakia, Poland, Ukraine, USSR, Yugoslavia, South Africa and Saudi Arabia.

67. Mary Ann Glendon, *A World Made New* (Random House, 2001), p. 58; Gérard Israël, *René Cassin* (Desclée de Brouwer, 1990), p. 204.

68. Gillian D. Triggs, *International Law: Contemporary Principles and Practices* (Butterworth, 2006), pp. 884–5.

69. Glendon, *World Made New*, pp. 51, 56.

70. Ibid., p. 65.

71. Ibid., p. 47. Interestingly, both Humphrey and Cassin wanted to include a statement of duties in the Declaration: ibid., p. 76.

72. I have based this chapter in part on a lecture, 'The Role of Leadership in the Creation and Maintenance of the Rule of Law', which I gave in the Middle Temple Hall on 21 February 2007 to celebrate the four hundredth anniversary of the Settlement at Jamestown.

CHAPTER 3. THE ACCESSIBILITY OF THE LAW

1. *Hamilton v Mendes* (1761) 2 Burr 1198, 1214.

2. *Vallejo v Wheeler* (1774) 1 Cowp 143, 153.

3. 'Economics and the Rule of Law: Order in the Jungle', *The Economist*, 13 March 2008, pp. 95–7, quoted by Tim Cowen, General Counsel and Commercial Director, BT Global Services, in '"Justice Delayed is Justice Denied": The Rule of Law, Economic Development and the Future of the European Community Courts', a paper prepared for the World Justice Forum on the Rule of Law held in Vienna in July 2008.

4. *Black-Clawson International Ltd. v Papierwerke Waldhof-Aschaffenburg AG* [1975] AC 591, 638 D.

5. *Fothergill v Monarch Airlines Ltd.* [1981] AC 251, 279 G.

6. *Sunday Times v United Kingdom* (1979) 2 EHRR 245, 271, para. 49.

7. Murray Gleeson, 'Courts and the Rule of Law', Melbourne University, 7 November 2001.

8. Hansard, H.C., 11 July 2007, col. 1455.

9. Anthony King, *The British Constitution* (Oxford University Press, 2007), p. 176, referring to a report of the Hansard Society Commission on the Legislative Process, *Making the Law* (Hansard Society, London, 1992), pp. 19, 291.

10. Rose LJ in *R v Lang* [2005] EWCA Crim 2864, [2006] 1 WLR 2509, paras. 16 and 53.

11. Rose LJ in *R (Crown Prosecution Service) v South East Surrey Youth Court* [2005] EWHC 2929 (Admin), [2006] 1 WLR 2543, para. 14.

12. The Renton Report on the Preparation of Legislation (1975).

13. Criminal Cases Review Commission, Annual Report and Accounts, 2007/8, p. 16.

14. *R v Chambers* [2008] EWCA Crim 2467, 17 October 2008.

15. Ibid., para. 28.

16. 'A Kafkaesque Excuse for Ignorance of the Law', *Guardian*, 3 November 2008, p. 12.

17. Ewoud Hondius, 'Sense and Nonsense in the Law', 28 November 2007, Inaugural Address when accepting the Chair in European Private Law, University of Utrecht, Kluwer-Deventer, 2007, p. 23, citing Joseph Kimble, 'Answering the Critics of Plain Language', *Scribes Journal of Legal Writing*, 5(1994–5), pp. 51–85

18. *Harrow London Borough Council v Qazi* [2003] UKHL 43, [2004] 1 AC 983; *Kay and others v Lambeth London Borough Council, Leeds City Council v Price* [2006] UKHL 10, [2006] 2 AC 465; *Doherty and others v Birmingham City Council* [2008] UKHL 57, [2008] 3 WLR 636.

19. Supreme Court Act 1981, s. 59.

20. By Dr Roderick Munday, of Peterhouse, Cambridge.

21. The first such occasion was in *R v Forbes* [2001] 1 AC 473, but this followed an isolated precedent thirty years earlier in *Heaton's Transport (St Helens) Ltd. v Transport and General Workers Union* [1973] AC 15, 94.

22. *R v Withers* [1975] AC 842, 854, 860, 863, 867, 877; *R v Rimmington* [2005] UKHL 63, [2006] 1 AC 459, para. 33.

23. Now enshrined in Article 7 of the European Convention on Human Rights.

24. J. D. Heydon, 'Judicial Activism and the Death of the Rule of Law', *Quadrant* (January–February 2003).

25. *Algemene Transport-en-Expeditie Onderneming van Gend en Loos NV v Nederlandse Belastingadministratie* [1963] ECR 1; *Costa v ENEL* [1964] ECR 585.

26. Treaty of European Union, art. 234.

27. I have based this chapter in part on a lecture entitled 'What is the Law?' delivered in Wellington, New Zealand, on 4 December 2008 in honour of Lord Cooke of Thorndon.

CHAPTER 4. LAW NOT DISCRETION

1. Lord Hewart of Bury, *The New Despotism* (Ernest Benn, 1929), p. 13.

2. *Vestey v Inland Revenue Commissioners* [1979] Ch 177, 197, per Walton J.

3. *Scott v Scott* [1913] AC 417, 477.

4. *D v National Society for the Prevention of Cruelty to Children* [1978] AC 171, 239 G.

CHAPTER 5. EQUALITY BEFORE THE LAW

1. Epistle to the Galatians, 3: 28. My quotation is taken from the Authorized (King James) Version of the Bible.

2. Acts of the Apostles, 16: 22–40; 22: 24–30; 25: 10–12.

3. Thomas Rainborough (or Rainborowe), 29 October 1647, in C. H. Firth (ed.), *The Clarke Papers*, Camden Society, New Series, 49 (1891), vol. 1, p. 301.

4. *Somerset v Stewart* (1772) Lofft 1, 20 ST 1.

5. F. Shyllon, *Black Slaves in Britain* (Oxford University Press, 1974), chaps. 6, 7 and 8; P. Fryer, *Staying Power: The History of Black People in Britain* (Pluto, 1984), pp. 120–26; J. Oldham, 'New Light on Mansfield and Slavery', *Journal of British Studies*, 27 (1988), p. 45; E. Fiddes, 'Lord Mansfield and the Sommersett Case' (1934) 50 *LQR*, p. 499; W. Wiecek, '*Somerset*: Lord Mansfield and the Legitimacy of Slavery in the Anglo-American World', *University of Chicago Law Review*, 42 (1974–5), p. 86; A. Samuels, 'What Did Lord Mansfield Actually Say?' (2002) 118 *LQR*, pp. 379–81.

6. See Tom Bingham, '"The Law Favours Liberty": Slavery and the English Common Law', University of Essex and Clifford Chance Lecture, 2003, pp. 15–16.

7. *Cartright's case*, 1569.

8. A. T. Denning, *Freedom Under the Law* (Stevens, 1949), p. 7; and *Landmarks in the Law* (Stevens, 1984), pp. 218–19. Lord Denning relied on, but misquoted, Lord Campbell's *Lives of the Chief Justices of England* (John Murray, 1849), vol. 2, p. 419.

9. Shyllon, *Black Slaves*, pp. 91–3; *Somerset v Stewart* 20 ST 1, col. 23.

10. The *ODNB* entry is by Ruth Paley.

11. Representation of the People (Equal Franchise) Act 1928.

12. *R v Secretary of State for the Home Department, ex p. Khawaja* [1984] AC 74, 111–12.

13. *A v Secretary of State for the Home Department* [2004] UKHL 56, [2005] 2 AC 68.

14. Ibid., paras. 64–5, quoting 'Counter-Terrorism Powers: Reconciling Security and Liberty in an Open Society' (February 2004), Cm. 6147, para. 36.

15. David Cole, *Enemy Aliens* (The New Press, New York, 2003), p. 85.

16. *Railway Express Agency Inc. v New York* 336 US 106, 112–13 (1949).

CHAPTER 6. THE EXERCISE OF POWER

1. David Blunkett, *The Blunkett Tapes* (Bloomsbury, 2006), p. 607.

2. *Holgate-Mohammed v Duke* [1984] AC 437, 443 D.

3. *R v Derbyshire County Council, ex p. Times Supplements Ltd.* (1991) 3 Admin LR 241, 253 A.

4. *R v Secretary of State for the Environment, ex p. Hammersmith & Fulham London Borough Council* [1991] 1 AC 521, 598 D–G.

5. *R v Secretary of State for the Home Department, ex p. Pierson* [1998] AC 539, 591 E.

6. *Padfield v Minister of Agriculture, Fisheries and Food* [1968] AC 997, 1030 B–D.

7. *R v Tower Hamlets London Borough Council, ex p. Chetnik Developments Ltd.* [1988] AC 858, 872.

8. *Porter v Magill* [2001] UKHL 67, [2002] 2 AC 357.

9. *R (Smeaton) v Secretary of State for Health* [2002] EWHC 886 (Admin), [2002] 2 FLR 146, para. [67].

10. *Nottinghamshire County Council v Secretary of State for the Environment* [1986] AC 240, 247 G.

11. *Secretary of State for Education and Science v Tameside Metropolitan Borough Council* [1977] AC 1014, 1064 E.

12. *In re W (An Infant)* [1971] AC 682, 700 D–E.

13. *Boddington v British Transport Police* [1999] 2 AC 143, 175 H.

14. e.g. *R (A) v Liverpool City Council* [2007] EWHC 1477 (Admin), para. [39]; *R v Secretary of State for the Home Department, ex p. Freeman*, 2 June 1998.

15. Lord Hailsham of St Marylebone, *Hamlyn Revisited: The British Legal System Today* (Stevens, 1983), p. 49.

CHAPTER 7. HUMAN RIGHTS

1. Paul Craig, 'Formal and Substantive Conceptions of the Rule of Law: An Analytical Framework' [1997] PL 467, 473–4.

2. J. Raz, 'The Rule of Law and its Virtue', in Raz, *The Authority of Law: Essays on Law and Morality* (Oxford University Press, 1979), pp. 211, 221.

3. 'Order in the Jungle', *The Economist*, 15 March 2008, p. 96.

4. Geoffrey Marshall, 'The Constitution: Its Theory and Interpretation', in Vernon Bogdanor (ed.), *The British Constitution in the Twentieth Century* (Oxford University Press, 2003), p. 58.

5. *Engel v The Netherlands (No. 1)* (1976) 1 EHRR 647, 672, para. 69. And see *Golder v United Kingdom* (1975) 1 EHRR 524, 589, para. 34.

6. See, for example, *Commission Communication to the Council and Parliament*, 12 March 1998, COM (98) 146.

7. Human Rights Committee, General Comment 14, (1994) 1 IHRR 15–16.

8. The House of Lords summarized the European case law in *R (Middleton) v West Somerset Coroner* [2004] UKHL 10, [2004] 2 AC 182, para. 2.

9. Ibid., para. 3.

10. *R (Amin) v Secretary of State for the Home Department* [2003] UKHL 51, [2004] 1 AC 653.

11. *Pratt v Attorney-General for Jamaica* [1994] 2 AC 1, departing from *Riley v Attorney-General of Jamaica* [1983] 1 AC 719.

12. *Ireland v United Kingdom* (1978) 2 EHRR 25.

13. *Selmouni v France* (1999) 29 EHRR 403, para. 101; *A v Secretary of State for the Home Department (No. 2)* [2005] UKHL 71, [2006] 2 AC 221.

14. *Napier v Scottish Ministers* [2005] 1 SC 229.

15. *R v Secretary of State for the Home Department, ex p. Cheblak* [1991] 1 WLR 890, 894.

16. *A v Secretary of State for the Home Department* [2004] UKHL 56, [2005] 2 AC 68.

17. *Secretary of State for the Home Department v JJ and others* [2007] UKHL 45, [2008] 1 AC 385.

18. *R (Gillan) v Commissioner of the Police of the Metropolis* [2006] UKHL 12, [2006] 2 AC 307.

19. *Austin v Commissioner of Police of the Metropolis* [2007] EWCA Civ 989, [2008] QB 660, [2009] UKHL 5, [2009] 1 AC 564; R. Clayton and H. Tomlinson, *The Law of Human Rights* (2nd edn., Oxford University Press, 2009), para. 10.53.

20. 22 Henry 8, cap. 9.

21. *Handyside v United Kingdom* (1976) 1 EHRR 737, para. 48; *Silver v United Kingdom* (1983) 5 EHRR 347, para. 97.

22. *Institutes: Commentary upon Littleton, Third Institute* (1628), cap. 73.

23. House of Lords, date unknown. Brougham's *Statesmen in the Time of George III*, First Series (1845).

24. Harry Snook, *Crossing the Threshold: 266 Ways the State Can Enter Your Home* (Centre for Policy Studies, 2007).

25. *Malone v Metropolitan Police Commissioner* [1979] Ch 344; *Malone v United Kingdom* (1984) 7 EHRR 14; Interception of Communications Act 1985.

26. *Wainwright v Home Office* [2003] UKHL 53, [2004] 2 AC 406, para. 26. That was a pre-Convention case, and the claimant established a breach of Article 8 in the European Court: *Wainwright v United Kingdom* (2007) 47 EHRR 40.

27. *R (Daly) v Secretary of State for the Home Department* [2001] UKHL 26, [2001] 2 AC 532.

28. *R (Razgar) v Secretary of State for the Home Department* [2004] UKHL 27, [2004] 2 AC 368.

29. Motor-Cycle Crash Helmets (Religious Exemption) Act 1976, re-enacted in the Road Traffic Act 1988 and the Motor-Cycle (Protective Helmets) Regulations 1980; Employment Act 1989.

30. *R v Williams* (1979) 1 Cr App R (S) 5; *R v Dandi and Daniels* (1982) 4 Cr App R (S) 306.

31. *R (Williamson) v Secretary of State for Education and Employment* [2005] UKHL 15, [2005] 2 AC 246.

32. *R (SB) v Governors of Denbigh High School* [2006] UKHL 15, [2007] 1 AC 100.

33. *McCartan Turkington Breen v Times Newspapers Ltd.* [2001] 2 AC 277, para. 1.

34. *Sunday Times v United Kingdom* (1979) 2 EHRR 245, disapproving a decision of the House of Lords. The House of Lords' majority decision in *Harman v Secretary of State for the Home Department* [1983] 1 AC 280 would, it seems, also have been disapproved had the application in *Harman v United Kingdom* (1984) 38 DR 53 not been settled.

35. *Tolstoy Miloslavsky v United Kingdom* (1995) 20 EHRR 442.

36. *Young, James & Webster v United Kingdom* (1981) 4 EHRR 38.

37. *Secretary of State for the Home Department v JJ and others*, above (n. 17), para. 20.

38. *R (Baiai and another) v Secretary of State for the Home Department (Nos. 1 & 2) (Joint Council for the Welfare of Immigrants and another intervening)* [2008] UKHL 53, [2009] 1 AC 287.

39. *Rasmussen v Denmark* (1984) 7 EHRR 371, para. 34; *James v United Kingdom* (1986) 8 EHRR 123, para. 74.

40. *Kjeldsen, Busk Madsen and Pederson v Denmark* (1976) 1 EHRR 711, para. 56; *R (Clift) v Secretary of State for the Home Department* [2006] UKHL 54, [2007] 1 AC 484, para. 27.

41. See Clayton and Tomlinson, *Law of Human Rights*, 2nd edn., para. 17.136.

42. *Belgian Linguistic Case (No. 2)* (1968) 1 EHRR 252, para. 3.

43. *Kjeldsen, Busk Madsen and Pederson v Denmark*, above (n. 40).

44. *Valsamis v Greece* (1996) 24 EHRR 294.

45. *Campbell and Cosans v United Kingdom* (1982) 4 EHRR 293, para. 36.

46. See *Guardian*, 11 April 2009, p. 36.

CHAPTER 8. DISPUTE RESOLUTION

1. John Cook, *Unum Necessarium: or, the Poore Man's Case* (1648), p. 66; quoted by Christopher Hill, *Liberty Against the Law* (Allen Lane, 1996), p. 266.

2. E. J. Cohn, 'Legal Aid for the Poor: A Study in Comparative Law and Legal Reform', (1943) 59 LQR 250, 253, n. 8.

3. R. Egerton, 'Historical Aspects of Legal Aid', (1945) 61 LQR 87.

4. The history is briefly summarized in Tom Bingham, 'Lecture at Toynbee Hall on the Centenary of its Legal Advice Centre', in *The Business of Judging* (Oxford University Press, 2000), pp. 391–407.

5. Cohn, 'Legal Aid for the Poor', p. 256.

6. By Tim Cowen, in his paper 'Justice Delayed is Justice Denied' for the World Justice Forum in Vienna, 2–5 July 2008, p. 11, n. 21.

7. *Hamlet*, Act 3, scene 1, l. 72.

8. See *Oxford Dictionary of National Biography*, entry for 'John Scott' by E. A. Smith.

9. In *Darnell v United Kingdom* (1993) 18 EHRR 205, a claim for unfair dismissal, the proceedings had lasted nearly nine years. In *Robins v United Kingdom* (1997) 27 EHRR 527, it had taken four years to resolve a dispute about costs.

10. Cowen, 'Justice Delayed', p. 18.

11. Ibid., pp. 24, 25.

12. Ibid., p. 19.

CHAPTER 9. A FAIR TRIAL

1. See, for example, *Engel v The Netherlands (No. 1)* (1976) 1 EHRR 647, para. 91.

2. T. Goriely, 'The Development of Criminal Legal Aid in England and Wales', in R. Young and D. Wall (eds.), *Access to Criminal Justice: Legal Aid, Lawyers and the Defence of Liberty* (Blackstone Press, 1996), p. 29.

3. (1904), vol. 1, chap. IV, p. 34.

4. See Tom Bingham, 'Lecture at Toynbee Hall on the Centenary of its Legal Advice Centre', in *The Business of Judging* (Oxford University Press, 2000), pp. 394–95.

5. See Lord Hewart of Bury, *The New Despotism* (Ernest Benn, 1929), p. 119.

6. Ibid., p. 124.

7. Tom Bingham, 'Judicial Ethics', in *The Business of Judging*, p. 77; D. Edwards, 'Judicial Misconduct and Politics in the Federal System: A Proposal for Revising the Judicial Councils Act)', (1987) 75 Calif LR.

8. Philip Ayres, *Owen Dixon* (The Miegunyah Press, Melbourne, 2003), pp. 235–8, 249–50, 258–9; and see 121 LQR (2005), p. 158, quoting the Solicitor General for New South Wales in the *Sydney Morning Herald*, 21 June 2003.

9. Anthony Lewis, reviewing *The Nine: Inside the Secret World of the Supreme Court* by Jeffrey Toobin in *New York Review of Books*, 20 December 2007, p. 61.

10. *Brown v Board of Education of Topeka et al.* 347 US 483 (1954).

11. Stephen Ambrose, *Eisenhower the President* (Allen and Unwin, 1984), p. 190.

12. Ibid.

13. *Davidson v Scottish Ministers* [2005] SC (HL) 7.

14. *R v Bentley, decd.* [2001] 1 Cr App R 307, 334.

15. *R v Horseferry Road Magistrates' Court, ex p. Bennett* [1994] 1 AC 42, 68, repeated in *Attorney General's Reference (No. 2 of 2001)* [2003] UKHL 68, [2004] 2 AC 72, 85, para. 13.

16. *Brown v Stott* [2003] 1 AC 681, 719.

17. Article 6(3) of the European Convention.

18. *R v Hayward* [2001] EWCA Crim 168, [2001] QB 862; *R v Jones (Anthony)* [2002] UKHL 5, [2003] 1 AC 1.

19. *Guardian*, 8 September 2008, p. 16.

20. This summary is based on the decision of the House of Lords in *R v H* [2004] UKHL 3, [2004] 2 AC 134.

21. *R v Davis* [2008] UKHL 36, [2008] AC 1128.

22. This, broadly, is the effect of Part 31.6 of the Civil Procedure Rules.

23. *Ventouris v Mountain* [1991] 3 All ER 472, 475.

24. The current procedure is well summarized by Paul Matthews and Hodge Malek QC in *Disclosure* (3rd edn., Sweet & Maxwell, 2007), pp. 327–45.

25. *D v National Society for the Prevention of Cruelty to Children* [1978] AC 171.

26. *R (Roberts) v Parole Board* [2005] UKHL 45, [2005] 2 AC 738.

27. *In re K (Infants)* [1965] AC 201, 237.

28. *In re D (Minors) (Adoption Reports: Confidentiality)* [1996] AC 593, 603.

29. See *Roberts*, above (n. 26), paras. 16–17.

30. Ibid., para. 19.

31. Ibid., para. 70.

32. Ibid., para. 78.

33. Ibid., para. 88.

34. Ibid., para. 97.

35. Ibid., paras. 19, 76–8, 83, 112, 144.

36. Ibid., para. 144.

37. Prevention of Terrorism Act 2005.

38. *Secretary of State for the Home Department v MB* [2006] HRLR 878, [2007] QB 415, [2007] UKHL 46, [2008] 1 AC 440.

39. *Secretary of State for the Home Department v AF* [2007] EWHC 651 (Admin), [2007] UKHL 46, [2008] 1 AC 440.

40. *M v Secretary of State for the Home Department* [2004] EWCA Civ 324, [2004] 2 All ER 863; *MB* and *AF*, above (nn. 38, 39).

41. *R v H*, above (n. 20), para. 22.

42. *M v Secretary of State for the Home Department*, above (n. 40), para. 13; *Roberts*, above (n. 26), para. 60.

43. *Secretary of State for the Home Department (Respondent) v AF (Appellant) and another (Appellant) and one other action (No. 3)* [2009] UKHL 28.

44. I have based this chapter in part on a lecture ('A Fair Trial') given to the Constitutional and Administrative Bar Association on 4 November 2008.

CHAPTER 10. THE RULE OF LAW IN THE INTERNATIONAL LEGAL ORDER

1. Ministerial Code, July 2007, para. 1.2.

2. S/2004/16, 23 August 2004, para. 6.

3. W. Bishop, 'The International Rule of Law', *Michigan Law Review*, 59 (1961), p. 553.

4. Charles Rhyner, Opening Statement before Boston Conference on World Peace through Law, 27 March 1959.

5. Simon Chesterman, 'An International Rule of Law?', *American Journal of Comparative Law*, 56/2 (2008), pp. 331–61 at p. 355.

6. Millennium Declaration, GA Res 55/2, UN Doc A/RES/55(2) (2000).

7. I have followed the formulation in Article 38 of the Statute of the International Court of Justice (1945).

8. *International Law* (Oxford University Press, 2007), p. 18.

9. Ibid., p. 20.

10. Ibid., p. 19.

11. Ibid.

12. Ibid., pp. 21–2.

13. Douglas Hurd, *The Search for Peace* (Warner Books, 1997), p. 6.

14. See *King's Prosecutor, Brussels, Office of the v Cando Armas* [2005] UKHL 67, [2006] 2 AC 1; *Dabas v High Court of Justice in Madrid, Spain* [2007] UKHL 6, [2007] 2 AC 31; *Pilecki v Circuit Court of Legnica, Poland* [2008] UKHL 7, [2008] 1 WLR 325; *Caldarelli v Judge for Preliminary Investigations of the Court of Naples, Italy* [2008] UKHL 51, [2008] 1 WLR 1724.

15. Chesterman, 'An International Rule of Law?', p. 348.

16. In *Golder v United Kingdom* (1975) 1 EHRR 524, para. 54.

17. Judge Mark Villiger, in a paper based on his oral contribution at the first International Law in Domestic Courts colloquium, held in The Hague on 28 March 2008, paras. 2(a) and (b).

18. *Ukraine-Tyumen v Ukraine*, 22 November 2007, para. 49.

19. *Erich Stauder v City of Ulm-Sozialamt* [1969] ECR 419, para. 7.

20. Antonio Tizzano, 'The Rule of the ECJ in the Protection of Fundamental Rights', in A. Arnull, P. Eeckhout and T. Tridimas (eds.), *Continuity and Change in EU Law: Essays in Honour of Sir Francis Jacobs* (Oxford University Press, 2008), 126–38, at p. 138.

21. Ibid., p. 138.

22. [1977] QB 529.

23. [1983] AC 244.

24. 'International Law in the House of Lords and the High Court of Australia 1996–2008: A Comparison', The First Michael Kirby Lecture in International Law, Canberra, 27 June 2008.

25. [1999] 2 AC 629.

26. [2006] UKHL 46, [2007] 1 AC 412.

27. *Adan v Secretary of State for the Home Department* [1999] 1 AC 293; *Horvath v Secretary of State for the Home Department* [2001] 1 AC 489.

28. *A v Secretary of State for the Home Department* [2004] UKHL 56, [2005] 2 AC 68.

29. *R (Al-Jedda) v Secretary of State for Defence (JUSTICE intervening)* [2007] UKHL 58, [2008] 1 AC 332.

30. *Minister for Immigration and Ethnic Affairs v Teoh* (1995) 183 CLR 273; *R (European Roma Rights Centre) v Immigration Officer at Prague Airport (UNHCR intervening)* [2004] UKHL 55, [2005] 2 AC 1; *R v Asfaw (UNHCR intervening)* [2008] UKHL 31, [2008] AC 1061; *Re Minister for Immigration and Multicultural Affairs, ex p. Lam* (2003) 214 CLR 1.

31. (Hart Publishing, 2005), chap. 1, pp. 3–26.

32. *The Invention of Peace & the Reinvention of War* (Profile Books, 2002), p. 1.

33. Article 24(1).

34. R. Peerenboom, 'Human Rights and the Rule of Law: What's the Relationship?', *Georgetown Journal of International Law*, 36 (2004–5), pp. 809–945, at pp. 936–7.

35. Philippe Sands, *Lawless World* (Allen Lane, 2005), p. 182.

36. Mark Danner, *The Secret Way to War* (New York Review of Books, 2006), pp. 129, 134.

37. Ibid., p. 91; Advice to the Prime Minister, 'Iraq: Resolution 1441', 7 March 2003.

38. Sir Michael Wood KCMG, Hersch Lauterpacht Memorial Lecture 2006, Third Lecture, 'The Security Council and the Use of Force', 9 November 2006, para. 9.

39. 'The pax Americana and the Law', first published in the JUSTICE journal in 2004, republished in extended form in 2007. In his oral presentation he used the word 'risible', which he later changed.

40. Sands, *Lawless World*, p. 189.

41. Lowe, *International Law*, p. 273.

42. Vaughan Lowe, 'Is the Nature of the International Legal System Changing? – A Response', *Austrian Review of International and European Law*, 8 (2003), pp. 69–73, at p. 72.

43. In communications to the author.

44. Article 43 of the 1907 Hague Regulations.

45. Ibid., Art. 46.

46. This subject is valuably discussed by Professor Sir Adam Roberts in 'Transformative Military Occupation: Applying the Laws of War and Human Rights', *American Journal of International Law*, 100/3 (July 2006), pp. 580–622.

47. See *R (Al-Skeini and others) v Secretary of State for Defence (The Redress Trust and others intervening)* [2007] UKHL 26, [2008] 1 AC 153, para. 6, case 6.

48. Memorandum by John Yoo and Robert Delabunty to William Haynes of 9 January 2002; Memorandum by Jay Bybee to Alberto Gonzales and William Haynes of 22 January 2002; Memorandum by Alberto Gonzales to President George W. Bush of 25 January 2002; Memorandum by the President

to the Vice-President and others of 7 February 2002: see Karen Greenberg and Joshua Dratel (eds.), *The Torture Papers: The Road to Abu Ghraib* (Cambridge University Press, 2005), pp. 38–79, 81–117, 118–21, 134–5. The development of the administration's policy on 'enhanced interrogation techniques' is traced by Professor Philippe Sands, *Torture Team: Deception, Cruelty and the Compromise of Law* (Allen Lane, 2008).

49. Memorandum by Jay Bybee (largely drafted by John Yoo) to Alberto Gonzales of 1 August 2002; see Greenberg and Dratel (eds.), *Torture Papers*, pp. 172–217, at pp. 213–14; see also Jane Mayer, *The Dark Side* (Doubleday, 2008), pp. 151–2, 224, 231.

50. Greenberg and Dratel (eds.), *Torture Papers*, pp. 383–404; *ICRC Report on the Treatment of Fourteen 'High Value Detainees' in CIA Custody*, www. nybooks.com.

51. Greenberg and Dratel (eds.), *Torture Papers*, pp. 405–556.

52. Ibid., pp. 987–1131.

53. Ibid., pp. 1132–64.

54. Memorandum by John Yoo to Alberto Gonzales of 1 August 2002, quoted ibid., at pp. 220–21.

55. 'The Rule of Law: Some Sceptical Thoughts', 16 October 2007, pp. 6–7.

56. 'Armed Intervention in the 1956 Suez Canal Crisis: The Legal Advice Tendered to the British Government', (1988) 37 ICLQ 773.

57. This chapter closely follows the text of a Grotius lecture ('The Rule of Law in the International Order') given on 17 November 2008 to mark the fiftieth anniversary of the establishment of the British Institute of International and Comparative Law.

CHAPTER 11. TERRORISM AND THE RULE OF LAW

1. William J. Brennan, Jr., 'The Quest to Develop a Jurisprudence in Times of Security Crises', *Israel Yearbook of Human Rights*, 18 (1988), 11, at 11.

2. *Ireland v United Kingdom* (1978) 2 EHRR 25.

3. Speech to the Council on Foreign Relations, 10 February 2003.

4. *Bell v Maryland* 378 US 226, 346 (1964), (Black J, dissenting).

5. Arthur Chaskalson, 'The Widening Gyre: Counter-Terrorism, Human Rights and the Rule of Law', *Cambridge Law Journal*, 67 (2008), pp. 69–91, at p. 74, footnotes omitted.

6. See K. J. Greenberg, 'Secrets and Lies', *Nation*, 26 December 2005, p. 39, at p. 40.

7. John F. Murphy, *The United States and the Rule of Law in International Affairs* (Cambridge University Press, 2004), p. 192.

8. David Bonner, *Executive Measures, Terrorism and National Security: Have the Rules of the Game Changed?* (Ashgate, 2007), pp. 4, 352.

9. 'Blair: Shackled in War on Terror', *Sunday Times*, 27 May 2007.

10. See, for instance, Phillip Bobbitt, *Terror and Consent: The Wars for the Twenty-First Century* (Allen Lane, 2008).

11. John Selden, *Table Talk* (1892), p. 131; see John Gray, *Lawyer's Latin* (Hale, 2002), p. 125.

12. Quoted by A. C. Grayling, *Towards the Light* (Bloomsbury, 2007), p. 6.

13. Conor Gearty, 'Human Rights in an Age of Counter-Terrorism', Oxford Amnesty Lecture, 23 February 2006.

14. *New York Review of Books*, 12 June 2008, pp. 68–71.

15. US PMO entitled 'Detention, Treatment, and Trial of Certain Non-Citizens in the War Against Terrorism', White House Press Release, 13 November 2001.

16. See Intelligence and Security Committee Report on *Rendition* (Cm. 7171, July 2007), para. 53.

17. *R v Horseferry Road Magistrates' Court, ex p. Bennett* [1994] 1 AC 42.

18. *R v Mullen* [2000] QB 520.

19. See *United States v Alvarez-Machain* 504 US 655 (1992)

20. ISC Committee Report, above (n. 16), para. 35.

21. Presidential Decision Directive 39, 'Counterterrorism Policy', 21 June 1995.

22. ISC Committee Report, above (n. 16), para. 35.

23. See Chaskalson, 'The Widening Gyre', pp. 83–4; David Cole and Jules Lobel, *Less Safe, Less Free: Why America is Losing the War on Terror* (The New Press, New York, 2007), p. 25; Craig Barlow, 'The Constitutional Tree: Rendering the Branches', *Amicus Curiae*, 70 (Summer 2007), pp. 17–21; David Cole, 'The Man Behind the Torture', *New York Review of Books*, 6 December 2007, pp. 38–43, at p. 38; Stephen Grey, *Ghost Plane* (Hurst & Co., 2006), chap. 4; *El Masri v Tenet* 437 F Supp 2d 530 (E. D. Va 2006), 2007 US App LEXIS 4796 (4th Cir. 2 March 2007).

24. Cole and Lobel, *Less Safe, Less Free*, p. 25.

25. See Irwin Cotler, 'Lessons of History', 2007 Raoul Wallenberg International Human Rights Symposium: Conference Proceedings, pp. 9–14; Chaskalson, 'The Widening Gyre', pp. 84–5; Cole and Lobel, *Less Safe, Less Free*, pp. 23–4; Grey, *Ghost Plane*, chap. 3.

26. Cm. 7171, paras. 65–6, 111–47; Grey, *Ghost Plane*, pp. 210–71.

27. *R (Al-Rawi and others) v Secretary of State for Foreign and Commonwealth Affairs and another (United Nations High Commissioner for Refugees intervening)* [2006] EWCA Civ 1279, [2008] QB 289.

28. Cm. 7171, p. 49, conclusion Y.

29. Government Response to the Intelligence and Security Committee's Report on Rendition (Cm. 7172, July 2007), pp. 6–7.

30. David Cole, *Enemy Aliens* (The New Press, New York, 2003), p. 58.

31. Cole and Lobel, *Less Safe, Less Free*, p. 107.

32. 'Counter-Terrorism Powers: Reconciling Security and Liberty in an Open Society' (February 2004), Cm. 6147, para. 36.

33. Cole, *Enemy Aliens*, p. 25.

34. Cole and Lobel, *Less Safe, Less Free*, p. 38.

35. Cole, 'The Brits Do It Better', p. 68.

36. Conor Gearty, *Guardian*, 18 November 2005.

37. Sarah Mendelson, *Closing Guantánamo*, Report of the CSIS Human Rights and Security Initiative and the Working Group on Guantánamo and Detention Policy, September 2008, p. 4.

38. Cole, *Enemy Aliens*, p. 42.

39. Cole and Lobel, *Less Safe, Less Free*, pp. 103–7.

40. 542 US 466 (2004).

41. 548 US 557 (2006).

42. 'Honour Bound to Defend Freedom? The Guantanamo Bay Litigation and the Fight for Fundamental Values in the War on Terror', [2008] *EHRLR*, Issue 4, pp. 433–53.

43. 553 US (2008).

44. *R v Governor of Durham Prison, ex p. Hardial Singh* [1984] 1 WLR 704.

45. (1996) 23 EHRR 413.

46. Bonner, *Executive Measures*, p. 220.

47. *A v Secretary of State for the Home Department* [2004] UKHL 56, [2005] 2 AC 68.

48. Bonner, *Executive Measures*, p. 239.

49. *Secretary of State for the Home Department v JJ and others* [2007] UKHL 45, [2008] 1 AC 385.

50. *Secretary of State for the Home Department v AF* [2007] UKHL 46, [2008] 1 AC 440; *Secretary of State for the Home Department v E and another* [2007] UKHL 47, [2008] 1 AC 499.

51. Chaskalson, 'The Widening Gyre', p. 86.

52. Police and Criminal Evidence Act 1984, ss. 43–51.

53. Sch. 8 to Terrorism Act 2000.

54. Sch. 8 to Terrorism Act 2000, as amended by s. 306 Criminal Justice Act 2003.

55. Sch. 8 to Terrorism Act 2000, as amended by s. 23 Terrorism Act 2006.

56. Eric Metcalfe, 'The Future of Counter-Terrorism and Human Rights', JUSTICE, 2007, p. 22.

57. *Charkaoui v Minister of Citizenship and Immigration and Minister of Public Safety and Emergency Preparedness* [2007] SCC 9, 276 DLR (4th) 594, para. 53.

58. Ibid., para. 64.

59. Ibid.

60. Ibid., para. 65.

61. This is the argument developed in Cole, *Enemy Aliens*; this account is based in particular on pp. 169–79.

62. *Detroit Free Press v Ashcroft* 303 F 30 681, 683 (6th Cir. 2002).

63. Cole and Lobel, *Less Safe, Less Free*, pp. 35–7.

64. 548 US 557 (2006).

65. David Luban, 'Tortured Evidence', 2007 Raoul Wallenberg International Human Rights Symposium: Conference Proceedings, p. 99.

66. Cole and Lobel, *Less Safe, Less Free*, p. 36.

67. Ibid.

68. Ibid.; Andrew Sullivan, 'We Don't Need a New King George', *Time*, 16 January 2006.

69. Luban, 'Tortured Evidence', p. 100.

70. Ibid.

71. Chaskalson, 'The Widening Gyre', p. 81.

72. *Ireland v United Kingdom*, above (n. 2).

73. *Selmouni v France* (1999) 29 EHRR 403, para. 101.

74. *A and others v. Secretary of State for the Home Department (No. 2)* [2005] UKHL 71, [2006] 2 AC 221.

75. Hansard, H.C., 24 May 2007, col. 1433.

76. Letter of UK Government Agent to the European Court of Human Rights, 24 January 2006 in *Ramzy v Netherlands*, Appn no. 25424/05.

77. *Saadi v Italy* [2007] 44 EHRR 50.

78. Ibid., para. 137.

79. Metcalfe, 'Future of Counter-Terrorism', pp. 13–14; Bonner, *Executive Measures*, pp. 256, 316–18.

80. *RB (Algeria) v Secretary of State for the Home Department, OO (Jordan) v Secretary of State for the Home Department* [2009] UKHL 10, 18 February 2009.

81. *Agiza v Sweden*, Communication No. 233/2003, UN Doc CAT/C/34/ D/233/2003 (2005), paras. 4.12, 13.4.

82. Cole and Lobel, *Less Safe, Less Free*, pp. 3, 31–2, 41.

83. Ibid., p. 62; *ACLU v NSA/Central Sec. Ser.* 438 F. Supp. 2d 754 (E D Mich 2006).

84. Interview, 19 May 1977.

85. Cole and Lobel, *Less Safe, Less Free*, pp. 135–6.

86. Ibid., p. 261.

87. Interception of Communications Act 1985.

88. Report of the Interception of Communications Commissioner (The Rt. Hon. Sir Paul Kennedy) for 2006, HC 252 (January 2008), paras. 12, 22, 58.

89. Henry Porter, 'Why I Told Parliament: You've Failed Us on Liberty', *Observer*, 9 March 2008, p. 33.

90. Timothy Garton Ash, 'The Threat from Terrorism Does Not Justify Slicing Away Our Freedoms', *Guardian*, 15 November 2007, p. 33.

91. Jonathan Oliver, 'The 1000 Ways the State Can Break into Your Home', *Sunday Times*, 20 July 2008, p. 13.

92. Garton Ash, 'Threat from Terrorism', p. 33.

93. Porter, 'Why I Told Parliament', p. 33.

94. Guidelines on Human Rights and the Fight Against Terrorism, adopted by the Committee of Ministers, 11 July 2002, at the 804th Meeting of the Ministers' Deputies, p. 5.

95. The Berlin Declaration: the ICJ Declaration on Upholding Human Rights and the Rule of Law in Combating Terrorism.

96. C. Dawson, *The Judgement of the Nations* (Sheed and Ward, London, 1943), p. 8.

CHAPTER 12. THE RULE OF LAW AND THE SOVEREIGNTY OF PARLIAMENT

1. Anthony Trollope, *The West Indies and the Spanish Main*, vol. 1, chap. IX, 1859 (Trollope Society edn., p. 120).

2. *The Sovereignty of Law: The European Way*, Hamlyn Lectures 2006 (Cambridge University Press, 2007), p. 5.

3. Ibid., p. 8.

4. Vernon Bogdanor, 'The Sovereignty of Parliament or the Rule of Law?', Magna Carta Lecture, 15 June 2006, p. 20.

5. Notably Professor T. R. S. Allan, in *Law, Liberty and Justice: The Legal Foundations of British Constitutionalism* (Oxford University Press, 1993), and in 'Parliamentary Sovereignty: Law, Politics, and Revolution', (1997) 113 LQR 443.

6. Lord Woolf, 'Droit Public – English Style', (1995) PL 57, although this view was later qualified ('Judicial Review – the Tensions Between the Executive and the Judiciary', (1998) 114 LQR 579); Sir John Laws, 'Law and Democracy', (1995) PL 72, and 'The Constitution, Morals and Rights', (1996) PL 622.

7. *R (Jackson) v Attorney General* [2005] UKHL 56, [2006] 1 AC 262, per Lord Steyn para. 102, Lord Hope of Craighead paras. 104–9, Baroness Hale of Richmond, para. 159.

8. Vernon Bogdanor, *Politics and the Constitution: Essays on British Government* (Dartmouth, Aldershot, 1996), p. 5; 'Our New Constitution', (2004) 120 LQR 242, 259.

9. J. L. De Lolme, *The Constitution of England, or An Account of the English Government* (1796).

10. A. V. Dicey, *An Introduction to the Study of the Law of the Constitution*, 10th edn. (1959), ed. E. C. S. Wade (Macmillan), p. 43.

11. See *Pickin v British Railways Board* [1974] AC 765; *R (Jackson) v Attorney General*, above (n. 7), para. 27.

12. *Salomon v Commissioners of Customs and Excise* [1967] 2 QB 116, 143, per Diplock LJ.

13. These examples, given by F. A. Mann, 'Britain's Bill of Rights', (1978) 94 LQR 512, 513, and Allan, *Law, Liberty and Justice*, pp. 130, 282, 285, are cited by J. Goldsworthy, *The Sovereignty of Parliament* (Oxford University Press, 1999), p. 260.

14. (1610) 8 Co Rep 113b, 118a; 77 ER 646, 652.

15. Goldsworthy, *Sovereignty of Parliament*, p. 111.

16. Ibid., p. 123.

17. Ibid., p. 112.

18. Ibid., p. 126.

19. Ibid., pp. 122–4.

20. Ibid., pp. 61; 127; 121, 157; 126, 200; 128; 151; 156; 181; 183; 189; 199; 201; 216; 44; 233; 1, 7, 9.

21. *Ex p. Canon Selwyn* (1872) 36 JP 54, per Cockburn CJ and Blackburn J.

22. J. J. Park, *The Dogmas of the Constitution: Four Lectures on the Theory and Practice of the Constitution* (1832), pp. 14–15.

23. William Rawle, *View of the Constitution of the United States* (1829).

24. *Algemene Transport-en-Expeditie Onderneming van Gend en Loos NV v Nederlandse Belastingadministratie* [1963] ECR 1; *Costa v ENEL* [1964] ECR 585.

25. *R v Secretary of State for Transport, ex p. Factortame Ltd. (No. 2)* [1991] 1 AC 603; *R v Secretary of State for Employment, ex p. Equal Opportunities Commission* [1995] 1 AC 1.

26. Human Rights Act 1998, s. 10.

27. 'Rights Brought Home', Cm. 3782, 1 October 1997, para. 2.13.

28. *A v Secretary of State for the Home Department* [2004] UKHL 56, [2005] 2 AC 68, para. 42.

29. S. 5(6) of the Northern Ireland Act 1998. There is no equivalent provision in the Government of Wales Act 1998, because the Welsh Assembly has no legislative competence.

30. See *R (Jackson) v Attorney General*, above (n. 7), per Lord Hope of Craighead at paras. 104–9, and the references given there.

31. See, for instance, Goldsworthy, *Sovereignty of Parliament*, pp. 165–73; Tom Mullen, 'Reflections on *Jackson v Attorney General:* Questioning Sovereignty', *Legal Studies*, 27/1 (2007), pp. 8–9.

32. *R (Jackson) v Attorney General*, above (n. 7).

33. Ibid., para. 102.

34. Ibid., para. 126.

35. Ibid., para. 159. Lord Carswell, para. 168, also described the principle of parliamentary sovereignty as a 'judicial product'.

36. Richard Ekins, 'Acts of Parliament and the Parliament Acts', (2007) 123 LQR 91, p. 103.

37. Particularly by H. L. A. Hart, *The Concept of Law* (Oxford University Press, 1961), chaps. 5–6; Goldsworthy, *Sovereignty of Parliament*, chap. 10.

38. Ibid., p. 3.

39. Ibid., p. 103.

40. See Lord Woolf, 'The Rule of Law and a Change in the Constitution', in Woolf, *The Pursuit of Justice* (Oxford University Press, 2008), pp. 128–9.

41. 'Parliament and the Courts', *Edinburgh Review*, 83/1 (1846), p. 40, ascribed to Lord Denman.

42. This chapter is largely based on a Commemoration Oration given at King's College on 31 October 2007: see *King's Law Journal*, 19 (2008), pp. 223–34.

EPILOGUE

1. LexisNexis, 2009.

2. *Rule of Law*, p. 80.

3. Ibid., pp. 111–15.

4. Ibid., p. 143.

5. Ibid., pp. 155–61.

6. Ibid., p. 165.

7. Ibid., pp. 166–8.

8. Epistle of James, 1: 22.

Index

He just wanted a decent book to read ...

Not too much to ask, is it? It was in 1935 when Allen Lane, Managing Director of Bodley Head Publishers, stood on a platform at Exeter railway station looking for something good to read on his journey back to London. His choice was limited to popular magazines and poor-quality paperbacks – the same choice faced every day by the vast majority of readers, few of whom could afford hardbacks. Lane's disappointment and subsequent anger at the range of books generally available led him to found a company – and change the world.

'We believed in the existence in this country of a vast reading public for intelligent books at a low price, and staked everything on it'
Sir Allen Lane, 1902–1970, founder of Penguin Books

The quality paperback had arrived – and not just in bookshops. Lane was adamant that his Penguins should appear in chain stores and tobacconists, and should cost no more than a packet of cigarettes.

Reading habits (and cigarette prices) have changed since 1935, but Penguin still believes in publishing the best books for everybody to enjoy. We still believe that good design costs no more than bad design, and we still believe that quality books published passionately and responsibly make the world a better place.

So wherever you see the little bird – whether it's on a piece of prize-winning literary fiction or a celebrity autobiography, political tour de force or historical masterpiece, a serial-killer thriller, reference book, world classic or a piece of pure escapism – you can bet that it represents the very best that the genre has to offer.

Whatever you like to read – trust Penguin.